UNDERCOVER
USER EXPERIENCE

★

Learn how to do great UX work
with tiny budgets, no time,
and limited support

CENNYDD BOWLES AND JAMES BOX

Undercover User Experience Design
Cennydd Bowles and James Box

New Riders
1249 Eighth Street
Berkeley, CA 94710
510/524-2178
510/524-2221 (fax)

Find us on the Web at www.newriders.com
To report errors, please send a note to errata@peachpit.com

New Riders is an imprint of Peachpit, a division of Pearson Education
Copyright © 2011 by Cennydd Bowles and James Box

Editor: Wendy Sharp
Production Coordinator: Tracey Croom
Copyeditor: Jacqueline Aaron
Compositor: Danielle Foster
Indexer: Emily Glossbrenner, FireCrystal Communications
Cover design: Mimi Heft
Interior design: Kathleen Cunningham

ISBN 10: 0-321-71990-5
ISBN 13: 978-0-321-71990-4

9 8 7 6 5 4 3 2 1

Printed and bound in the United States of America

★ ENDORSEMENTS

"A wonderful, practical, yet subversive book. Cennydd and James teach you the subtle art of fighting for—and designing for—users in a hostile world."

—Joshua Porter, co-founder Performable & co-creator of 52WeeksofUX.com

"Cennydd and James's clever and crafty book will teach you how to make your own rules, play well with others, and create a culture of UX from the ground up."

—Whitney Hess, user experience design consultant, author of the blog Pleasure and Pain

"Making design matter in your organization is not about titles and talk. It's about what you get done every day. *Undercover User Experience Design* will show you the way."

—Luke Wroblewski, author of *Web Form Design & Site-Seeing*

"At Clearleft we pride ourselves on delivering exceptional design even with tight deadlines and budgets. This indispensable guide to guerrilla UX explains how we do it."

—Andy Budd, co-founder and managing director of Clearleft

★ ACKNOWLEDGMENTS

Cennydd and James thank

Wendy Sharp, Jacqueline Aaron, Tracey Croom and all the staff at Peachpit, for helping a couple of novices to achieve something we still find unimaginable. Your dedication, patience and irreplaceable advice kept us going. We hope we've done justice to your efforts.

Our colleagues past and present at Clearleft—Paul Annett, Sophie Barrett, Andy Budd, Kate Bulpitt, Natalie Downe, Andy Hume, Jeremy Keith, Paul Lloyd, and Richard Rutter—for creating an environment in which we could flourish, and covering for us when deadlines got tight. Special thanks to James Bates for going beyond the call of duty with designerly assistance.

Whitney Hess, Luke Wroblewski and Josh Porter for their flattering endorsements, and Peter Boersma, Dan Brown, Leah Buley, Leisa Reichelt and Brandon Schauer for kindly agreeing to let their ideas be featured. You all exemplify the intelligence and generosity of this fabulous community.

Chris Summerlin (www.honeyisfunny.com) for his fantastic chapter illustrations, and for demonstrating superior knowledge of classic cars.

Francis Storr for his invaluable comments on the early drafts of this book, and helping us to see through our readers' eyes.

Cennydd thanks

The Brighton and London UX communities, for inspiring and tolerating me. Particular respect to Martin Belam, Desigan Chinniah, Danny Hope, Johanna Kollmann and Matthew Solle for their tireless undercover work for the British UX community. Thanks also to Ian Fenn for the sticky note tip, to Amanda Jahn and Sjors Timmer for their offers of support, and to my mentorship partners for asking the smart questions that gave birth to this book.

Friends—Sascha Auerbach, Alex Block, Tom Britten, Chloe Brooks, Isla Buchanan, Sharon Chesworth, Justin Clark, Rebecca Cottrell, Joe Cross, Pippa Dakin, Jo Denyer, The Sharp Foundry, Andy Fox, Kushal Gaya, Sélène Hinton, Kate Howson,

Emily Kawasaki, Sam Lewis, Tom Payne, Jos Roberts, Rejina Juie Sabur, Dan Waddy, Matt Wheeler, James Wilson, Craig Wood, James Woods and many more—for their support and forgiving my enforced social hibernation.

My family, for—well—pretty much everything.

Anna, for her support and compassion. Words aren't enough.

My co-author James. Heartfelt thanks and eternal respect. Although I still prefer the provisional title for the book.

James thanks

The UX community, especially my allies in Brighton and the rest of the British Isles. Thank you for inspiring me. Keep sharing.

All my friends. For remembering me during my somewhat prolonged absence, but more importantly, for reminding me "It's just a book."

My family. For their unerring support and encouragement. I hereby promise you cake.

Sarah, Jemima & Charles. Without your extraordinary patience and understanding none of this would be possible. I love you.

And finally, Cennydd. An incredible talent and someone I feel honored to call my co-author and friend.

TABLE OF CONTENTS

GOING UNDERCOVER

We won't tell you why user experience matters. You already know.

Every day, you use bad products. Websites that don't make sense. Doors that open the wrong way. Things built the easy way or the cheap way, rather than the right way.

Fortunately, it needn't be like this. Designers across the globe are shaping a movement—user experience (UX) design—that puts people first and creates products that are usable, useful, and enjoyable. UX design is a harmless infection, but once you catch it, the world changes. Everything can be made better.

Some businesses understand the benefits of user experience design and are seeing the rewards. However, for every company that appreciates UX design, thousands don't. They're not necessarily bad companies; they've survived tough times by keeping costs down and efficiency high. However, they're focused on themselves or their competitors—design and usability aren't priorities. Most people work for a company like this. Perhaps you do, too.

The fundamentals of UX design—creating personas, making wireframes, usability testing—are easy to learn but difficult to put into practice. Your business has its way of doing things, and perhaps user experience isn't in your job description. It's hard to know whether you can make a difference, and where to start trying.

We feel your pain. Nowadays, we're lucky enough to work with clients who value UX design, but it wasn't always that way. We had to sneak user experience into companies by stealth and make enthusiasts of people who'd previously never cared about design. Today, we meet, mentor, and train many people who face the same challenges we did. Again and again, we find what stops these people from doing great UX work isn't their lack of knowledge, but their inability to apply that knowledge in businesses that don't "get it."

You can overcome these challenges, if you're prepared to make the effort. This book covers the stealthy, practical approach we believe in. We call it Undercover User Experience Design. Here's the manifesto.

★ THE UNDERCOVER MANIFESTO

We believe in **going undercover**. We don't mean you should skulk around in the dark. As an undercover user experience designer, your mission is to get people excited about UX without them realizing what you've done. Unless you're an expensive consultant or a senior manager, you won't do this by knocking on the CEO's door and demanding change. User experience design is disruptive. It asks difficult questions. Good-enough managers in good-enough companies don't want you to rock the boat; they're busy worrying about meeting next month's targets.

We believe in **introducing UX from the ground up**. Sneak UX into your daily work, prove its value, and spread the message. Results are more persuasive than plans.

We believe **change comes through small victories**. Putting users at the heart of a business is a huge cultural change. It takes years. But you'll be surprised what you can achieve with focus, patience, and persistence.

We believe in **delivery, not deliverables**. Some people practice *user-scented* design, not *user-centered design*. They churn out documents—sitemaps, wireframes, specifications—but they're not interested in what happens next. UX is a mindset, not a process—it lasts all the way until the site is live, and after.

We believe **good design today is better than great design next year**. There's no such thing as perfection in design, particularly on a medium as fluid as the web. You're not here to impress other designers; your job is to make your users' lives better.

We believe in **working with people, not against them**. Just as we empathize with users, we must respect and understand our colleagues. We reject elitism and accept that compromise is healthy. Passion is fine; zealotry is not.

We believe in **action, not words**. Introducing UX into your company is a lot of work. No one will do it for you, so you'd better get cracking. Remember, it's often easier to get forgiveness than permission.

THE WEB AND BEYOND

This book is unapologetically focused on web UX design, since the web industry employs an abundance of user experience specialists, ourselves included. However, undercover UX techniques suit a wide range of media including mobile applications, desktop software, and other digital products. Please substitute your preferred medium as required.

EXPLORING THE PROBLEM

The experts will tell you that great user experience comes from crystal-clear strategy and exemplary leadership. They're right of course, but that doesn't help us much right now. As a UX aficionado in a company that doesn't share your passion, you're not going to be able to have that kind of impact right off the bat.

Starting the UX conversation at your organization by asking difficult abstract questions isn't likely to be effective. It's easy to point out deficiencies, but what senior managers want is for people to show initiative. So take a pragmatic view, start small and focus on achieving results through UX. Succeed and you'll gain the ammunition to kick the UX discussion off in the right way. Instead of expressing subjective complaints, you'll be able to benchmark your site experience against competitors, uncover unknown problems, and highlight areas for improvement.

★ HIT THE GROUND RUNNING

So let's follow the advice of our manifesto and get right into the action. Here are some undercover UX techniques you can use today that don't need money or lots of time. You won't even need official clearance—just find some spare time and do them. These techniques offer a great chance to show the value of UX and will give you a headstart on the hard work that lies ahead.

EXPERT REVIEW

Estimated time: Two hours.

An expert review—also known as a **heuristic evaluation** or simply a **site review**—involves a structured appraisal of your website, exploring UX issues using rules of thumb known as heuristics.

Choose the most important user tasks on your site and step through the various pages involved, considering the points in our heuristic list below. This list gives guiding principles that lie behind a good website, along with some questions to prompt your analysis. It's based on the work of human-computer interaction experts such as Jakob Nielsen, Rolf Molich, and Bruce Tognazzini, but streamlined for undercover UX work.

The questions listed here are a starting prompt only; don't be afraid to add more. You can either give your site a score for each heuristic or just record any issues you come across.

Undercover UX heuristics

A good website is:

- Made for humans. Is the site relevant and useful? Is it enjoyable? Does it match users' **mental models**—that is, their understanding of how the site should work? Does the site speak in user-friendly language? Does it offer the right level of user control?

- Forgiving. Does the site prevent errors? When errors do occur, are they clearly explained and easy to recover from? Does the site minimize the user's mental workload?

- Accessible. Is the text legible? Does the site cater to color-blind users? Is there unnecessary animation? Does the site work with assistive technology such as screen readers?

- Self-evident. Is it clear what and who the site is for? Is it easy to navigate? Is the layout logical, with the most important information prominent? Do the icons and graphics make sense?

- Predictable. Is the site consistent? Does it use known web conventions? Are there good defaults for user input? Does the site remember user preferences?

- Efficient. Are text, imagery, and structure concise? Is the site responsive, giving good feedback? Does it prioritize the most important tasks?

- Trustworthy. Is the site accurate? Is its content up-to-date? Are there any bugs? Does the site keep its promises?

The prescriptive nature of expert reviews can feel artificial, but they're an excellent way to analyze your site against tested design principles. They also help build your familiarity with the site and, by conducting them at regular intervals, you can see whether the site is improving.

COMPETITIVE ANALYSIS

Estimated time: one or two days.

A logical next step is to conduct expert reviews on competitor sites. Use the same list as before and add further detail about competitor sites' functionality, structure, content, and visual style. You can also extend this analysis to well-designed sites that aren't direct competitors, to act as an aspirational benchmark. Screen shots can help illustrate your thoughts and, if you're giving scores, plot them on charts for simple comparison ■.

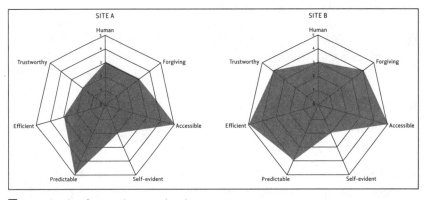

■ *Use radar plots for a quick way to show how your site compares to competitors.*

Competitive analysis, twinned with an expert review, is a perfect conversation starter. What do other sites offer that you don't? What do you offer that they don't? What opportunities arise? Do your competitors use different language? Are they after the same types of customer?

Competitive analysis can reveal valuable information about the business landscape, but remember it's only a small step in the UX design process. Don't get hung up on competitors. If you're always chasing their tails, how will you ever get ahead?

ANALYTICS SNAPSHOT

Estimated time: one to three days.

Site analytics ■ are a goldmine for undercover UX work, but they're often overlooked. Your first task is of course to find out whether you already have analytics data. If you don't, it should be easy enough to make the case for gathering some:

entry-level tools such as Google Analytics (www.google.com/analytics) and Mint (www.haveamint.com) are free or very cheap, and require just a tiny snippet of JavaScript.

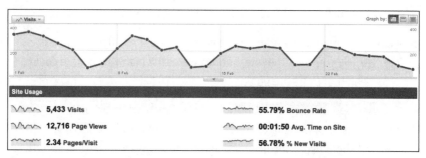

B *Analytics data tells you how people are using your site.*

Leave your analytics software to gather data for at least two weeks, then examine the following metrics for useful clues about how your site is being used and who your users are.

- Unique visitors: how many does your site have? Remember that the more visitors you have, the more diverse they are likely to be.

- New versus returning visitors: whose needs are you serving best?

- Visits per unique visitor: are people coming back regularly, or only using the site once?

- Day and time of visit: are users browsing on the weekends or during the working week?

- Location: are your visitors local or spread across the world?

- Entry pages: are people coming to your homepage or a page deep within your site?

- Bounce rate: what's the proportion of users who are leaving after seeing just one page? This figure gives a hint about the quality of your entry pages. A bounce rate of 60 percent or higher may be a cause for worry.

- Referring sites: how are users getting to your site anyway?

- Keywords: what phrases are people putting into search engines to find your site? Is your site the right destination for those keywords?

■ Navigation paths: are visitors finding the main areas of the site? How? Where are they going next?

■ Conversion rate: how many visitors are going on to become registered users? Or customers? How long does this take them?

■ Page views per visitor and time spent on site: are these figures increasing? Usually you want them to, but be aware that high values here could also mean that users are getting lost.

■ Browser, operating system, and screen resolution: what are people using? This data will suggest technical constraints and can also give subtle hints about users. If they're using the latest release of Mozilla Firefox, they're probably web-savvy. If they're using Microsoft Internet Explorer 6 at 1:00 p.m., they might be surfing on their lunch break. Call it a hunch rather than reliable data, but it can be helpful.

■ Registered users and paying customers: what proportion of your users comes from these valuable groups? Is that figure growing? Do these visitors use the site differently than first-timers? How many of your customers visit on any one day?

Search logs

If your site has an internal search function, spend some quality time with your search logs C. Search data can give you pointers about user intent, from which you can infer gaps in your content, reasons for visiting, success (or otherwise) of your navigation, and users' mental models of the site.

Search log	
Term	**Searches**
bill	1817
electricity	1100
tariff	665
billing	654
gas	590
estimated bill	521
payment	500
contact	486
customer services	481
green energy	469
dual fuel	461
pay bill	452
call center	452
cheap	429
energy prices	424

C Look at your search logs to see what people are trying to find.

You might be surprised by the most popular search terms on your site. Do they reflect your main business priorities? Is there any pattern to them—for example, seasonal variation? Do visitors use narrow search phrases such as "The Godfather Part II," or broad terms like "films"? Are people using negative keywords— keywords they want omitted from their search, as in "godfather -films"—to clean up search results? Do any geographic terms crop up in your search logs?

You can run a rough test of the search system by trying the most popular terms yourself. Are the results relevant? Appropriately ranked? Overall, is search helping or hindering users?

Other analytics

There's plenty more data you can gather beyond regular site analytics. Click-tracking tools such as CrazyEgg (www.crazyegg.com) can help you monitor which links and page elements are attracting attention, by creating a heat map of user clicks. Social media activity can also be revealing, and you may find that the marketing team is already monitoring it. Which pages on the site are people commenting on, retweeting, and saving on social bookmarking sites?

CONTENT AUDIT

Estimated time: one to five days.

We admit it: content audits are dull. However, if your site is content-heavy and informational, a content audit is the only way to fully understand the structure and quality of the content you offer, which in turn will help you tackle future information architecture (IA) and content challenges. A content audit is also useful for content teams, so partner with them if you can. It can act as the foundation of content strategy and hence provide a way to improve the site's content and how it's managed. For more on working with content teams, see Chapter 6, "Working with..."

Begin by taking a content inventory **D**. Step through your site and map out its structure in a spreadsheet, giving the title and URL of each page, and a short description of its contents (text, images, videos, links). Use indentation to represent the site hierarchy, and introduce a numbering scheme if your site is large enough. Bigger inventories will of course take longer to compile. For very large sites, you may only have time to analyze the first few levels, but try to explore at least a few branches to the end; it's often in the deep areas of the site that problems lie.

ID	Title	URL
\	\	**Content analysis: uxlondon.com**
1	Home	http://2010.uxlondon.com/
2	Speakers	http://2010.uxlondon.com/speakers/
3	Programme	http://2010.uxlondon.com/programme/
3.1	Wed 19th May	http://2010.uxlondon.com/programme/#day1
3.1.1	Design for Engagement	http://2010.uxlondon.com/programme/2010-05-19/designforengagement/
3.1.2	Search Patterns: The Future of Discovery	http://2010.uxlondon.com/programme/2010-05-19/searchpatterns/
3.1.3	Metrics-driven Design	http://2010.uxlondon.com/programme/2010-05-19/metricsdrivendesign/
3.1.4	Designing for Improvisation	http://2010.uxlondon.com/programme/2010-05-19/designingforimprovisation/
3.1.5	The Art & Science of Seductive Interactions	http://2010.uxlondon.com/programme/2010-05-19/seductiveinteractions/
3.1.6	Experiencing Comics	http://2010.uxlondon.com/programme/2010-05-19/experiencingcomics/
3.1.7	Making Movies is Hard Fun	http://2010.uxlondon.com/programme/2010-05-19/hardfun
3.2	Thu 20th May	http://2010.uxlondon.com/programme/#day2
3.2.1	User Interview Techniques	http://2010.uxlondon.com/programme/2010-05-20/interviews/
3.2.2	Information Architecture with Maps	http://2010.uxlondon.com/programme/2010-05-20/iawithmaps/
3.2.3	Knowledge Games: Design practices for systems thinking	http://2010.uxlondon.com/programme/2010-05-20/knowledgegames/
3.2.4	Real-World Agile User Experience Design	http://2010.uxlondon.com/programme/2010-05-20/agileux
3.2.5	How To Think With Pretty Pictures	http://2010.uxlondon.com/programme/2010-05-20/contentmodels/
3.2.6	Content Strategy: The Missing Piece of the UX Puzzle	http://2010.uxlondon.com/programme/2010-05-20/contentstrategy/
3.3	Fri 21st May	http://2010.uxlondon.com/programme/#day3

D *A content inventory helps you come to grips with your site's content.*

This simple inventory should help you understand exactly what you're dealing with and any obvious problems such as gaps, broken links, and inconsistent labeling.

For extra insight, you can build this inventory into a full content audit by adding detail. Take a closer look at the content of each page and comment on how well it meets the likely needs of both businesses and users. Make note of any content that is redundant, outdated or trivial, and provide a score if you wish. If possible, add a column to note who is responsible for this content and give some thought to how frequently the page should be reviewed. You can even enrich your content audit with analytics data. Are the good pages the ones that people are visiting? Are any critical pages hampered by broken links? Is what you're providing the same as what people are looking for?

BUILD THE BUZZ

Alongside these specific techniques, look for ways to share your passion for UX. Forward interesting articles to your teammates, point out novel interfaces on sites you see, or hold a lunchtime workshop to try out UX techniques. Do whatever it takes to get knowledge and enthusiasm into the business.

Also spend some time thinking of a suitable UX kickoff project, preferably something manageable and relatively low-risk to begin with. Perhaps it's creating personas, improving help pages, or prototyping a new sign-up process. Small projects make good choices since they provide a self-contained way to demonstrate the value of UX. Whatever you choose, write a short outline of the problem and a plan of what you'd like to do. If your subliminal infiltration is successful, eventually someone will officially tell you to "give this UX thing a shot." Having a project in mind means you can leap at that opportunity.

WHAT'S NEXT?

These quick undercover techniques won't give you a conclusive list of your site's UX problems, but they'll give you something to get your teeth into. They should at least get people talking about user experience, and might give you a good platform to volunteer for further UX work.

However, don't expect this quick skirmish to win you the war. To make a convincing case for lasting change, you'll need to learn more about the business, the site, and who's using it.

★ DEFINING THE PROBLEM

The design process is a complex beast. The experts all agree it's made up of several phases, but they disagree about what these stages are and where they overlap. Rather than open that can of worms, we'll just start with what we call the discovery phase, in which you explore what needs to be done and the context of the project.

The techniques we've covered helped you hit the ground running, but to make a real difference you should weave UX principles into the entire design process. Look around for a new project that needs some UX love, or take on your starter project as a quick win.

It will be tempting to jump at the chance to learn about users. Hold that thought. You'll get there soon, but we recommend you first spend time truly understanding the problem you're trying to solve. In his book *Unfolding the Napkin*, visual thinking maestro Dan Roam says, "Whoever is best able to describe the problem is the person most likely to solve it." He's right. This stage may not be glamorous, but time spent here will be repaid later.

DESIGN PROBLEMS

Design problems are typically framed in terms of *objectives, requirements,* and what we call *unrequirements.*

Objectives

Objectives answer the question "What do we want to achieve?" If you can become involved in setting project objectives that meet both business and user experience goals, your mission to embed UX is off to a shining start. Here are some example objectives that could be good for both businesses and users:

■ Reduce shopping-cart abandonment by 15 percent within a month

■ Increase customer repeat business by 10 percent by Christmas

■ Reduce log-in errors to 10 per day throughout February

Good objectives should be SMART: specific, measurable, achievable, realistic, and time-bound. Objectives therefore need **metrics**: measurements that help you know if the objective was met. These may be simple site-use statistics—unique visitors, shopping-cart abandonment rates—or broader, attitudinal data such as the Net Promoter Score.

THE NET PROMOTER SCORE

The Net Promoter Score (NPS) is a simple measure of customer satisfaction. Customers answer the question "How likely is it that you would recommend our company to a friend or colleague?" on a scale of 0 to 10. Using basic arithmetic, this data is turned into a percentage showing the ratio of "promoters" to "detractors". NPS provides a basic way to quantify a notoriously intangible thing—happiness—making it a useful metric for UX design.

Requirements

Requirements answer the question "How should we do it?" They're usually a delicate combination of what users want and what the business needs to earn a profit, and range from the highly specific ("Allow users to upload an image under 1MB") to the decidedly vague ("Keep my work safe!").

Unrequirements

If requirements are the "how to," unrequirements are the "how not to." They come in two forms: constraints and exclusions.

Constraints are usually imposed and immovable, while requirements are usually chosen and flexible. Constraints may come from many areas—deadlines, technology, regulations, and more—but they exist for every project. Projects with few constraints lend themselves to a more open-ended design, whereas tightly constrained projects require a more focused design. You may find you have a preference for one or the other, but both present interesting UX challenges.

Exclusions are approaches that the business deliberately wants to avoid. Perhaps they want to steer clear of areas that competitors dominate, or ignore feature requests that are too expensive or contravene company policy. Talking about exclusions not only saves effort later in the design process, but can also focus people's minds on the core essence of the product.

THE IMPOSSIBLE PROBLEM

To understand the problem, you just need to find out all the objectives, requirements, and unrequirements. Sound easy? Sadly, it's impossible. Objectives, requirements, and unrequirements are classic examples of what's known as "tacit knowledge," which can never be adequately stated in full. However thorough you are in the discovery phase, extra requirements and constraints will creep out once you start proposing solutions. Sometimes you simply need to see a design to understand why it won't work.

Design problems are also rife with subjectivity. Everyone has a unique opinion, which will often cause conflict. You might see your Marketing and IT departments locked in a bitter debate over whose requirements are correct, while the users are scratching their heads and asking for something altogether different. Not only that, but people change their minds. Objectives, requirements, and unrequirements appear from nowhere and vanish without warning. Customers start using a competitor, the economy collapses, or your new CEO wants to do things differently.

Since you can never fully understand the problem, you can never design the perfect solution either. Hopefully that's a liberating feeling; embrace it. In lieu of perfection, your job is to learn whatever you can about the objectives, requirements, and unrequirements of your users and business, and use this information intelligently in your design.

RESEARCHING THE BUSINESS

Unlike most users, businesses aren't afraid to make demands, so it's usually not difficult to discover business needs. These needs might be unnecessary, vague, or misdirected, but you should still bring them to the surface. Only when business needs are in the open can you explain how to marry them with the needs of users.

There are two main sources of business objectives, requirements, and unrequirements: the brief and stakeholders.

The brief

First, we need to know if you're an "innie" or an "outtie."

If you're an outtie, your client will have prepared a written brief. It'll give basic information about how your client sees the design problem and what they're hoping for in a solution. You'll find similar information in the Request for Proposal (RFP), or they may even be the same document. If you're an innie, there probably won't be a brief per se, but whoever kick-started the project will have created a business case

> **NOTE**
>
> Innie or outtie? Don't worry, it's not a personal question. An "innie" is someone who works in-house, and an "outtie" is an external consultant or agency employee. We'll use these terms a fair bit, so work out which term applies to you.

explaining their view of the problem and the benefits of solving it. This could be held in a formal project initiation document or simply an email.

The brief will never tell you the whole story, but getting your hands on it will save you valuable time in the discovery phase.

Stakeholder interviews

Every project has two types of stakeholder: people who can affect the project, and people whom the project affects. Both groups can help you understand business needs, so find out who your stakeholders are and talk to them, either in an informal chat or a scheduled interview.

It can be hard to arrange these conversations, particularly with senior stakeholders or people in different offices, but be politely persistent and be sure to talk with everyone who can affect the project's outcome. Poor access to stakeholders can seriously delay UX projects, and there's nothing worse than seeing your hard work wasted because you didn't talk to the right person in advance.

Here are some questions we ask stakeholders on our projects. Since we're outies, we ask for lots of background information, but we never ask all of these questions. Instead, we pick ones that are most relevant and add others as we see fit. You should too.

The organization

- What's the organization's history?
- What's the current standing of the organization?
- What are the organization's goals?
- Who are our competitors?
- What are our strengths and weaknesses compared with them?
- How is the organization structured?
- How do we want the organization to be seen?

The site

- What's the site for?
- What's the site's history?
- What does the site do well? Poorly?
- What technical platform does it run on?
- Does the site use a content management system (CMS)?
- What content management processes support the site?
- How much flexibility for technical change is there?
- How would you rate the site's usability? Structure? Content? Visual design?

Users

- Who are the current users?
- Are they the people the company is targeting?
- What characteristics do they have?
- Why do they use our site and not a competitor's?
- What do users say about our site?
- How do they use our site now?
- What do users need to do for us to be successful?

People

- What's your role in the project?
- Who else is working on the project?
- What are their roles?
- What is the decision-making/sign-off process? How long will it take?
- Who else do we need to talk to?

The project

- What problem will the project solve?
- What are the project's objectives?
- How do they relate to the overall business objectives?
- Why are we doing the project now?
- What specific project requirements do you have?
- What are the constraints (time, resources, technical, legal, and so on)?
- What's causing them?
- When do you think the project will be released?
- Have we tried anything like this before? What happened?
- Does anyone else do this well?

- What factors could make the project a success? Could we handle success?
- What issues could throw the project off course? Could we handle failure?
- How could we really screw this up?
- How will we measure success or failure?
- What's your gut feeling about the project?

Take thorough notes either by hand or, if possible, audio recording since you'll revisit these answers throughout the process. As you review your notes, look out for anything that sounds like an objective, a requirement, or an unrequirement.

★ CULTURE

The brief and your stakeholder interviews are a great start to the discovery phase, but the skilled undercover UX designer must also read between the lines.

Just like people, organizations have complex and varied personalities, so a design approach that works in one situation could fall flat on its face in another. It takes skill and practice to appreciate the cultural factors that affect design, but the rewards are substantial. Understand what makes the organization tick, and you can anticipate problems before they happen and tailor your approach accordingly; this is all the more important if you don't have the luxury of trying various strategies to see which fits.

Innies will already have a feel for the organizational culture. Outties should make finding it out a top priority. Look over the notes from your stakeholder interviews. What do people talk about most? Are stakeholders motivated by numbers? Or success stories? Are there any terms, phrases, or concepts that hint at the underlying corporate mentality? One useful exercise is to write down the adjectives you would use to describe the organization to a friend. *Innovative? Conservative? Angry? Efficient?* Then consider how these traits could affect your undercover UX quest. It can be helpful to take your adjectives to extremes and consider the impact they would have. For example, a "nimble" company could, at its worst, become flighty and unable to commit to an idea. This would suggest you should focus on execution and a defined sign-off process so that new ideas don't become a distraction.

RED FLAGS

With experience, you'll develop a sixth sense for cultural red flags, and learn ways to change your approach accordingly. Here are some warning signs we watch for in new projects.

Design disinterest

Many organizations simply don't care about design, or see it as an expensive luxury rather than a strategic investment. The website might have been made by hired hands, but ongoing design (if there is any) is undertaken by staff with little design training. Without clear ownership, the site usually degrades from its launch state until finally another redesign is grudgingly approved.

Thankfully, these organizations are ripe for a UX intervention. Done right, UX can set these companies apart from their competitors, helping them reach new customers, sell more, and pull ahead. However, you must make the value of this disruptive new approach clear—and the sooner the better, so that you yourself don't become fossilized into a particular role or mindset. So hit the ground running and keep pushing. Focus on small, winnable areas, supplementing them with case studies showing the difference design has made in similar companies, and you can demonstrate return on investment for UX work.

Cash cows

Cash cows are products or site sections that earn serious revenue. They're typically fueled by very high traffic, or they may be critical pages on sites with large, passionate user bases. Cash cows are protected zealously either by the business or users. As such, they're risky targets for undercover UX work. Unless you can prove you'll have a positive effect, you won't be allowed to make meaningful changes to that part of the site. You may prefer to aim for easier wins and build trust in your ability, but if you still want to take on the challenge of a cash cow, you'll need a low-risk approach. This means conducting thorough research to prove you understand user and business needs, heavy testing to make sure your design works (see Chapter 5), and carefully managing stakeholder and user concerns. Even with these safeguards, be ready to fail fast and don't get attached to your solutions. If they don't work, they'll be abandoned immediately.

Enormous expectations

If different stakeholders have conflicting expectations of the project, or it is seen as the savior of all the company's ills, trouble usually lies ahead. Sky-high expectations can cause disappointment, paralyzing fear of failure, and poor decisions. In these conditions, clarify expectations in advance, revisiting the objectives, requirements, and unrequirements, and agreeing on whose version is the one that matters. You may need to downplay particularly unrealistic expectations in light of your time or budget constraints and prioritize problems accordingly. Strong research can greatly help refocus people on customer needs rather than their own flights of fancy. Learning more about users increases your chance of getting things right and thus satisfying stakeholders' expectations.

Power problems

Every organization has its own approach to authority and sign-off. Some companies make decisions as a team, some as a dictatorship. Either extreme can make life difficult for UX designers. Flat power structures typically mean lots of stakeholders and the dreaded "design by committee," while a project with a dominant senior authority can mean you're subject to personal whim, even in the face of clear contradicting opinions from his staff and users. Power struggles between departments are equally dangerous: designers can be caught between these warring factions, causing frustration and wasting time. Finally, external designers are sometimes brought in "too low down the chart." As an outtie, you may have been hired by a middle manager: will this person actually have the final say?

Concerns about sign-off authority are awkward but should be raised early in the project, before they create too much tension. You should diplomatically clarify whose authority is final—you might have to ask senior managers—and ensure you have access to that person early in the project. You may need to involve her in your sign-off process or persuade her to delegate responsibility to a subordinate if she can't spare the time. You might also allow more time for review and sign-off if you foresee power problems.

Difficult deadlines

Does the organization want an exemplary site no matter how long it takes, or are there immovable deadlines for the project? If time constraints are unrealistic, find out what's driving them. External deadlines are usually enforced, but internal ones may be chosen for convenience. If deadlines are indeed fixed, be prepared to vary scope and pare functionality down to a minimum, postponing inessential requirements until a future release. You should also consider keeping your documentation quick and low fidelity, and heavily involving others in the design process so you don't become a bottleneck.

Paralyzing process

Large organizations in particular can be hamstrung by process. Did it take you weeks to get an access badge? Does the site have pressing legal implications? Does everything have to be put in writing? Process-heavy organizations are prone to the "That's not how we do things around here" syndrome, which quickly suffocates the user-centered spirit. The good news is that you can do a lot of UX work in these companies without anyone even noticing. Instead of taking on the futile challenge of proposing new processes, work quickly and stealthily so you can demonstrate successful results. It will still be an uphill struggle, but if senior staff in these organizations see UX design as good practice, they'll push for it to be integrated into the entire business. Convince these influential implementers of process and you're set for life.

Content confusion

Large informational sites hold an enormous amount of content, which needs careful curation and management. Unless thorough content strategy and pro-cesses are in place, these projects will cause painful content bottlenecks. Content management systems (CMSs) can relieve the labor but introduce extra technical constraints, so learn about the system you're using. Additionally, buddy up with content colleagues, put aside extra time to handle content provision, and phase content work early in the project. Ideally your project team will include a content strategist; if not, you may have to adopt the role and push content to the top of everyone's priority list (see Chapter 6).

CULTURE AND RELATIONSHIPS

Taking the time to talk with people, listen to them, and learn about your organi-zation's culture will help you not only to plan your work, but also to build relation-ships. You may have noticed that the stakeholder questions all spoke of "our" needs, not "yours." This is an important point, even if you're an external consul-tant. This attitude of ownership helps build a collaborative mindset.

You'll need to find allies to do effective undercover UX work, and it's easier to work with friends. If you genuinely understand and care about their concerns, they'll help your cause by contributing to design, committing to action, and co-owning the results. As we mentioned, UX requires asking difficult questions; it may create more work for your colleagues or erode some of their power. But if these people like and trust you, they'll be more receptive to ideas they'd otherwise resist.

★ USER RESEARCH UNDER THE RADAR

There aren't many shortcuts to all this business analysis, but it's essential. UX design requires a careful balance between the needs of business and customer, and without either half, the equation fails. So now that you've learned about the problem from the business perspective, it's time to find out how to thrill your users.

DO YOU NEED TO RESEARCH?

User research isn't an easy sell to most businesses. It has a reputation for being long, expensive, and hard to act upon. Some companies even claim it's a waste of time. Instead, they believe in "scratching your own itch"—that is, making software for your own needs. This is an excellent approach if you genuinely represent the target audience. In these situations, the design process flows naturally since you can answer questions and make clear decisions without recourse to research and testing. But most of us aren't the end users of our websites, so this approach only works in select circumstances.

Similarly, marketing specialists often think that design can be based on market research. On the surface, it's understandable: market research and user research both reveal valuable information about customers and how to reach out to them. However, they focus on different things. Market research is primarily about opinions: about a brand, about personal beliefs, or about a specific marketing approach. User research is about behavior: what drives people, how they do things, how and why they're likely to use your site.

So is market research useless for UX design? Certainly not. Most marketing teams really do care about the customer. They're usually very research-focused and as such possess mountains of data, which can help you understand who your users are. By supplementing this with user research to find out why and how they'll use the site, you can build a better picture of customers. So don't think of it as a research deathmatch where only one format can win; both market research and user research are relevant to both UX and marketing staff, and it can be a great way to build a relationship between the departments.

Sometimes it's true that user research is overkill. For small, low-risk projects it's better to get something out there and improve it through testing and trial and error. But on any decent-sized project where quality matters, user research will help.

GET PERMISSION OR GO UNDERCOVER?

As an innie, it might not be too hard to persuade the company to undertake user research. After all, most organizations see the importance of building up knowledge of the customer. However, if you're an outtie, you'll have a tougher time of it. Unless clients are already willing to pay for user research, they might deem it unnecessary—particularly if it's the consultant, rather than the business, that's going to benefit from the knowledge. To get agreement for user research in these circumstances, you need to be involved in writing proposals, going to pitches, and getting clients to talk about user experience.

Until then, or if you think asking permission will be more trouble than it's worth, you can conduct research under the radar. Undercover methods might cost you a few lunchtimes or a few favors, but they're worth the effort. On the upside, with these lightweight methods, you'll find your designs are much stronger and the case for UX should be firmer.

FINDING PARTICIPANTS

First, you'll need to find people to talk to. There are many ways to approach this.

Research recruiters

If money is no object, pay a research recruiting service. It'll help you define a target profile, find participants, and schedule sessions. However, it's expensive: often over $100 per user. If you have this kind of budget, don't hesitate to use it, but for most undercover work you'll probably want to recruit users yourself.

Existing customers

Talk with your customer service or sales teams to see if they could identify people who'll be willing to help—these could be local customers, or people farther afield if you don't mind doing some remote research.

Alternatively, you could approach people in your customer database. Emailing is a quick and cheap approach, but be careful of data protection law: in some countries, the customers will have had to consent to receiving emails first. If your site has user forums, or you know of other places online where your potential customers hang out, you might be able to approach people there, as long as you do so with the right attitude and treat the community with honesty and respect. You could also consider recruiting directly through your site: you can build a recruitment form either on the site itself or with a service such as Google Docs (http://docs.google.com) or Wufoo (www.wufoo.com), and direct a select group of users to the form by a link or a pop-up panel on your homepage.

Friends, family and colleagues

Friends and family may be appropriate undercover research participants if they're representative of the site's users. Ask around, or put the word out on Facebook, Twitter, and similar sites. However, keep an eye on who you're getting. It's easy to end up with people similar to yourself who don't really reflect the diversity of your users.

If you work in a large organization, you could try asking employees to participate in your undercover research. There will be a large pool of people to draw from with a wide range of technical literacy, but be aware that their domain knowledge may skew your results.

Public recruitment

Finally, you can resort to complete strangers. It's often surprisingly effective to pop to a local coffee shop and ask people for ten minutes in exchange for their coffee. The online equivalent is to post a message on a free classifieds site such as Craigslist. You'll probably want to use a short screener: a set of simple questions designed to filter out people who don't fit the profile for your research. In our experience, students, the unemployed, and stay-at-home parents tend to be over-represented when recruiting through classified ads, especially if you are asking them to be available during working hours.

Your knowledge of your user base will help you know whether public recruitment is appropriate. For sites with broad appeal, it can be easy and worthwhile, but if your site is aimed at a niche user base—for example, commercial pilots—you're wasting your time. For these specialists, go straight to your existing customers or find the money somehow and commission a recruiter.

If you're handling the recruitment alone, allow yourself sufficient time. You'll need to find people, assess their suitability, schedule mutually acceptable times, and sort out payment, so you'll need a couple of hours per user.

Incentives

Existing customers will often give up their time for free; being heard can be sufficient payoff. But for people who don't already have an emotional connection to your website, you'll need to provide an incentive.

This is usually driven by what you can come up with. Cash is ideal ($40 a hour and above), but you may find it easier to arrange gift vouchers, free subscriptions, or whatever your finance team or client will allow. If you're going with the coffee shop approach, bring cash and try your luck at persuading people to help in exchange for a cup of coffee and a muffin. Keep the receipts and claim them on expenses, but do clear this first so you don't end up paying out of your own pocket.

RESEARCH METHODS

All research methods have advantages and limitations, with some particularly suited to undercover work. Rather than blindly applying your favorite approach, become familiar with a range of methods and choose the right one based on your project's circumstances.

Corridor test

One of the simplest ways to find out more about users is to watch them using your existing site. (Since we also recommend you do this frequently with your own designs, we'll cover guerrilla usability testing in depth in Chapter 5.) A corridor test is so called because all it takes is a laptop and a passerby, assuming they're not heavily involved with the site. You can even ask employees in the lunchroom or agency colleagues working on other projects. Ask them to run through some critical tasks on the site. By watching how they use the site, you can uncover flaws with the existing system.

One-on-one interviews

The most obvious way to find out more about people is to talk with them. Interviews can tell you not only how customers might use your site, but also more about their lives, needs, and motivations.

A good interviewer uses a number of well-known techniques:

- Asking open-ended questions that encourage the participant to elaborate (who, what, where, when, why, and how questions are particularly useful)

- Avoiding leading questions that might distort responses (for example, "What's wrong with our website?")

- Clarifying understanding by paraphrasing what the participant says

> **TIP**
>
> If at all possible, and with the participant's permission, record interviews on a voice recorder or a laptop (free software such as Audacity and GarageBand is ideal). It's still worth bringing along a pen and paper to face-to-face interviews, since you or the participant might want to sketch out a particular point. Taking pictures or video with your cellphone is a great way to preserve these diagrams for future use.

However, the undercover interviewer needs another skill: the art of small talk. You won't have a great deal of time to plan sessions in detail, so you should be comfortable listening to people and getting them to open up. The more confident you are at talking to different types of people, the better you'll be at research interviews and truly listening to what people have to say. If small talk isn't your strong point, maybe it's an excuse go to more parties—for research purposes, of course.

Face-to-face interviews make it easier to build rapport, but they can take a lot of arrangement. If you need to talk to geographically remote users or don't have the time to travel around to meet people, remote interviews are an excellent undercover tool. You can either use the phone (make sure you're paying!) or, if your participants are technically proficient, voice over IP (VoIP) software such as

Skype. If you're holding a phone interview, it can be helpful if the participant is near a computer with internet access so you can refer to the site itself. Interviews can be tiring and generate large amounts of information that need processing, so try not to schedule more than three a day.

Group interviews and focus groups

If you're really pressed for time or can't arrange to meet people individually, group interviews can help. However, there's significant baggage to be aware of. The focus group, close cousin of the group interview, has a bad reputation among user researchers, since it's used mostly as a market research tool. Although the group format can be a helpful vehicle for user research, we strongly recommend avoiding the "focus group" label, which will instill certain presumptions and arouse suspicion in your marketing colleagues.

> **NOTE**
>
> A focus group is a form of qualitative research in which a representative group of people are led through a structured discussion in order to reveal their desires, opinions, and attitudes toward a product or service.

One of the major difficulties with group formats is ensuring that loud and opinionated participants don't overwhelm a group. As facilitator, you need to tactfully encourage others to have an equal say.

Don't even think of using a group interview to test an interface. Group interviews are tools for research, not evaluation. Save them for times you want to learn about the potential audience for a new idea and their responses to specific suggestions.

Contextual inquiry

Interviews have limitations, not least the problem of self-reporting. People naturally omit salient points or make inaccurate claims about their goals because of the challenges of remembering details and the unusual task of self-analysis. Contextual inquiry—studying people as they go about their daily lives —avoids these problems.

Contextual inquiry isn't really undercover: you can't exactly do it on your lunch break. But you still have options. Jump at the opportunity to go on site visits—perhaps with sales staff as they meet new prospects or with engineers when they go to customer sites. If possible, ask in advance if you can shadow an end user while you're there. Customers are often quite happy for you to do this, since it shows you're genuinely interested in trying to make a site that will benefit them. While shadowing, you'll mostly observe and take notes, but you may be able to ask some interview questions during a quiet moment, so pick some juicy ones. Two that we've found particularly useful are "What one thing could we do to make your life easier?" and "What other sites or companies do this well?"

> **NOTE**
> Contextual inquiry is a technique for examining and understanding how users interact with products or services in their natural environment. Using a combination of direct observation and interview, the technique provides detailed insight on tasks, pain points and user preferences.

While we're on the topic, *contextual inquiry* is one of those jargon phrases that we don't recommend you use too widely. *Direct observation* or *fly on the wall* is a good substitute.

Surveys

Surveys have the clear undercover advantages of being quick, cheap, and easy to analyze, even with lots of responses. Survey results are unambiguous and direct: unlike other methods, there's no need to "read the tea leaves"—meaning they often give clear and powerful evidence to support or disprove a particular belief. However, like other quantitative methods, surveys tell you the what, but not the why. They're best paired with qualitative methods like interviews.

Your survey should consist mostly of closed questions, yes/no responses, and Likert scales (such as a scale from "Disagree strongly" to "Agree strongly"), but you can also include more open-ended questions. Be aware that these will dramatically increase analysis time, so start with a small sample size so as not to overwhelm yourself, and seek more responses if you need further information.

Many organizations already conduct regular surveys, so instead of creating one from scratch, you may be able to piggyback one or suggest a collaborative survey with other teams who need customer feedback. Online tools such as Survey-Monkey (www.surveymonkey.com) can make your job easier, but make sure that your organization is comfortable with you using a third-party service, since data may be stored externally.

Customer feedback

Customer service representatives are the undercover UX designer's best friend. However large the organization, they're always closest to real users and can be an invaluable source of information about customer needs and issues.

Most customer service reps will be glad of the opportunity to share their knowledge, and a day spent shadowing front-line reps can teach you more than a week of focus groups. Customer service reps can also provide invaluable knowledge about patterns in customer types or behavior. For instance, do inquiries come from men or women? Are they typically new customers or repeat customers? What are their typical frustrations? How interested are they in different features of the company's products? In addition to talking to and shadowing customer service staff, ask whether the organization keeps a log of feature requests from customers. Some of these ideas will be extremely valuable. Some will be useless. Either way, a short time trawling through these requests can often give a clearer understanding of users' pain points.

Just bear in mind that customer feedback is by its nature exceptional. This data will show an inherent bias toward customers who have enough free time to contact the company, or those who are stuck and have gripes they need help with. Satisfied or busy users won't appear on the customer service radar.

Card sorting

A card sort is a tool for examining how people group topics. The technique is simple. Write down topics or site sections on index cards and ask your participants to group related items. In an open card sort, participants can group the cards freely, and then choose a label for each group. In a closed sort, cards must be grouped into predetermined categories. Card sorts are predominantly used to determine labeling and structure, but can also reveal deeper insights into people's expectations of content and functionality.

It's straightforward to add a card sort onto other research methods, especially interviews. Simply allow an extra 10 to 15 minutes at the end to explain the process, run the test, and note the results. Remote card sorting tools such as OptimalSort (www.optimalworkshop.com/optimalsort.htm) and WebSort (www.websort.net) let you run tests online, but we believe card sorting is better done in person if possible. Not only can you explain the rules of the game more effectively, but also you can question the participant about why they made certain choices.

Card sorting can help you understand how users form relationships between concepts, and allow you to create a shared vocabulary from the results. They can also generate surprisingly convincing quantitative data. Many card sort analysis templates—such as Donna Spencer's free template (www.rosenfeldmedia.com/books/cardsorting/blog/card_sort_analysis_spreadsheet)—include basic cluster analysis, which can give highly visual results **E**. Closed card sorts are easier to analyze than open ones.

No	Name	About	Services	Clients	Po
1	History	85			
2	Prices		55	30	
3	Location	100			
4	The team	45	45		
5	Consultancy		100		
6	Web analytics		75		
7	Workshops		75		
8	Clients			100	
9	Portfolio	5		25	
10	Contact	75			
11	Training		80		

E *Card sorts can give surprisingly quantifiable results.*

Third-party research

External research such as market reports can be a useful supplement to your knowledge. However, they're a poor substitute for firsthand user research. In the words of Jared Spool, outsourcing your research "is like outsourcing your vacation. It gets the job done, but not the results you were seeking."

For other external advice, consider reaching out to fellow specialists on UX mailing lists and blogs. Many will have encountered similar projects before or have sector experience that can aid your understanding. However, each project is different, so be wary of relying too much on third-party information. Also be sure to protect your client's confidentiality if you've signed a nondisclosure agreement (NDA).

Other research methods

Subject-matter experts (SMEs) within an organization will certainly have something to say about users and their habits. On occasion, they may get so caught up in the minutiae of the topic that they overlook bigger issues, but SMEs will have valuable knowledge of the end user, any noticeable clusters, and their likely behaviors. This can give you a great start, but try to back up their suggestions with first-hand research.

Some circumstances may call for you to use less popular research methods. In a **trigger word analysis**, you simply give users a representative task and ask what words or phrases they would look for on the user interface (UI). A task like "Learn about member discounts" might elicit words or phrases such as *benefits*, *money off, membership deals*, and so on; you can then analyze these results and ensure they are incorporated in your content strategy or UI itself.

Finally, for user interactions that happen over a long time, **diary studies** can prove useful. These involve asking users to record all their interactions with a particular product or task over a long time frame, such as a week. As such, they're not ideal for undercover work, but they can be useful if you need to know how people approach a complicated task that can't be done in one sitting. Where appropriate, cellphone cameras are excellent tools for turning a diary study into a photo journal.

RECORDING AND ANALYZING RESEARCH

After your research is complete, you need to put some time aside to analyze it. Revisit your recordings and notes, keeping an eye out for repeated themes. Do users talk about their goals? What are their likes and dislikes? Where are their needs not being met? Do they have any interesting alternative approaches? What language do they use to describe the domain? To parallel the business objectives, requirements, and unrequirements, draw up a similar list for users.

While you're analyzing your research, make a note of your techniques. Did you ask the right questions? Did you let the participant speak or constantly interrupt them? What worked? What didn't? What would you change next time?

There's no magic to research analysis except hard work, lots of sticky notes, and grouping. But, just like the business research, put in the effort here and your designs will be stronger and more likely to be useful.

HOW MUCH RESEARCH IS ENOUGH?

No matter how much research you have, a UX designer will always yearn for more. So it's best to let your project time line dictate how much effort to dedicate to research. If you only have, say, ten weeks, you won't want to be researching into week five. But don't panic if you can't do as much up-front research as you'd like. You can still learn about users later in the design process. We'll talk more about that in Chapter 5, "Refining Your Solution."

★ RESEARCH OUTPUTS

Most UX books advise that you pause at this stage to present your research to your stakeholders or client. But if you're undercover, we're not so sure.

The main reason to present your research is to get sign-off. Certainly if you asked for permission to conduct the research, you need to report back with your findings. Similarly, if people need to approve the objectives, requirements, and unrequirements you've gleaned, pause here to get consensus. But if you ran the research without the organization knowing, it's usually easier to convince people of the benefits of UX once you can show them designs—asking for blessing to continue opens up the possibility of denial. In this scenario, you should still analyze and summarize your research carefully, even if you don't share it yet. You'll need to back up your design decisions later, and the act of condensing research into a digestible format will help you focus on the most important issues.

But let's assume that you need to come up for air and show your work so far. In what formats should you present your research?

JUST THE EXECUTIVE SUMMARY

We don't recommend writing a big report. If your company's not particularly into design, your report could lie forever unread on someone's desk. That's not going to start the organization thinking about UX. Instead, write just the executive summary. Summarize both the business needs and the user needs—one or two pages should suffice—and circulate this among your key stakeholders.

The approach you take is important. Don't just mention the problems; talk about how you'll address them, too (hopefully using the techniques we'll cover in the next few chapters). Assume agreement instead of asking permission. "We have some problems; can I fix them?" shows less confidence and initiative than "I thought I'd look at the user experience of our site. We have some problems, so here's my plan to fix them." This may sound presumptuous, but think of it this way: If your dentist asked if he could treat you with a new procedure, what would you think? Probably "What's the downside?" and "Could this go wrong?" Now how about if he just told you instead? You'd let him get on with it and wonder why on earth he thought you'd care.

One or two pages isn't much, so you'll have to leave things out of this executive summary. That's fine. If people want to know more, they can talk to you in person. That's a big win for your cause. It means you get a chance to talk to people about UX, and it's much harder for them to shut down your enthusiasm and knowledge in person than it is on paper.

Whatever you include in the report, keep it personal and relevant. Although it can be useful to discuss general findings, individual stories can lend authenticity to your work. These could be stories you heard firsthand from research participants, or perhaps feedback from shadowing the customer service team. Quotations can be very persuasive, as can corridor test videos if you have them.

QUANTITATIVE DATA

Although your research findings are probably mostly qualitative, numerical data can add legitimacy to your findings. Analytics data can be displayed graphically, as can card sort clusters, usability test success rates, customer complaints, and, of course, surveys **F**. Some stakeholders will respond better to charts and numbers than words; hopefully your interviews and cultural analysis will have identified the people for whom you should take this approach. If you're dealing with a lot of quantitative data, it's worth learning some basic statistics so you can see the true patterns in your data, as well as how the data could be abused or misinterpreted.

USE OF STUDENT PORTAL

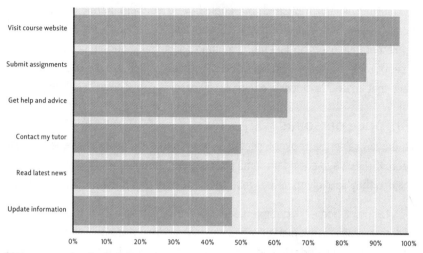

F *You can graphically display user responses gathered from a survey.*

PERSONAS

Personas are research-based documents that describe typical users. Each persona contains a name, photo, age, occupation and a brief description of the person, their traits and their habits **G**. Personas are the ideal tool to give everyone a shared view of genuine customers. Like secret agents synchronizing their watches, they give stakeholders a common reference point, helping people make decisions for customer needs, not their own. But they also have another benefit: they get people talking about user experience and how to design a website for customers. Exactly what we want.

G *A simple persona helps the team focus on users, not assumptions.*

Michelle teaches at a primary school in Summertown, Oxford. She rents a 2-bed terraced house nearby with her journalist fiancé John and her cat Benji.

She loves painting and runs an art club after school twice a week. She also helps make costumes for school productions.

She's fairly confident with using computers, and regularly keeps in touch with her friends on social networks. Michelle uses Internet Explorer 7 on a Dell laptop given to her by her school to surf the web. Her favourite sites are the BBC and Times Education Supplement.

Since Michelle is saving up for her wedding, she's keen to cut her household bills. She's therefore trying out price comparison websites to see where she can save money. In particular, she's keen to save on her car insurance, which has risen to £455 this year.

Michelle

31, Teacher, Oxford

"Why is car insurance so bloody expensive?"

Since Alan Cooper introduced the concept of personas in his book *The Inmates Are Running the Asylum*, thousands of people have tried them in their own organizations. It's now widely agreed that for best results, you should interview dozens of representative users and identify common goals, traits, and behaviors. Creating a set of robust research-driven personas can take weeks. But what if you don't have that luxury? Is it possible to make quick, cheap, undercover personas?

Cut-price personas

When you raise the topic of personas, your marketing team may question the need. If they've spent a long time working on a detailed market segmentation project, they're likely to query what personas offer that marketing data doesn't.

It's a fair point. Some UX designers see a clear dividing line between the two forms of data, explaining that market segments don't address the most important design issues such as why people come to the site and the role it will play in their lives. These designer argue that it's easier to design for a person (Joe, aged 34) than numbers (a group that's 78% male, aged 26-35), and that marketing data tells us little about people's mental models, the language they use, and so on.

In our undercover world, these differences are accurate in principle but petty in practice. Personas represent the other side of the marketing data coin. Segments cluster individuals into groups. Personas create individuals to represent groups. Since we prefer good design today to great design next year, marketing data is a decent starting point for cut-price personas.

Look at the marketing data the organization has gathered and you may be surprised at what it contains. Although demographic information will probably dominate, you may find information about other purchasing behaviors, sites that these users visit, and even psychographic information such as the VALS segmentation tool (www.strategicbusinessinsights.com/vals). Instead of instinctively rejecting this information, build on it, explaining that by creating a realistic persona to represent each segment you will be able to design a more effective site.

Of course, cut-price personas have limitations. Ideally, you should supplement them with firsthand research, surveys, analytics and any other information you can gather. However, UX designers are naturally skilled at evaluating information, understanding bias, and coming to even-handed solutions. Keep your wits about you, and you might find that cut-price personas suffice for your initial design work. We don't recommend you rely on cut-price personas for critical decisions, but they do a good job as a tool to get the organization talking. Your personas will already have the support of your marketing colleagues and your willingness to work with, not against, other teams will smooth the adoption of UX techniques.

Treat cut-price personas as living hypotheses; keep them sketchy to begin with, and slowly refine them as you build up your behavioral understanding of users throughout the project. Perversely, ambiguity can help your case for conducting user research: "Let's settle this by talking to people directly."

Another technique is to base a persona on someone you already know. Just like "scratching your own itch," this provides an unambiguous reference point, but it comes with dangers. The primary risk is that you'll become locked into that persona and, when confronted with more data, won't be able to evolve the persona in a different direction. Again, be aware of the limitations of this approach, and consider your persona a stand-in until you can talk with enough users to check its validity.

Persona tips

Choosing believable names and photos for your personas can take longer than you'd think. To save time, search on dating sites to find photos of suitably aged people—so long as your personas won't be made publicly available, of course. Then, calculate your persona's year of birth and pick a unique initial for their first name, to reduce the chance of people mixing up your personas. You can then use name charts (such as www.babynamewizard.com/namevoyager) to find popular names from that era.

If a full persona would be overkill, think creatively about how to achieve the same goal. Do your research participants write a blog, upload photos on Flickr, or post on Twitter? Could you take a snapshot and share it with the team? (Don't share anything personal, of course.)

Most stakeholders embrace personas since they give a personal view on the customer that's rarely seen. However, some stakeholders—usually the ones who rely on numerical evidence—consider personas too flimsy since they by necessity involve a little creative license. You will need to convince these people by showing the rigor of your research, rather than the output; the quantitative approaches mentioned above are likely to be more persuasive.

The other source of resistance is the refrain "But we want our website to work for everyone!" You can counter this with a thought experiment. Ask your stakeholder to imagine how they'd explain a complex concept, such as inflation, to a friend. They might choose to use pictures, words, or both. Then ask them to imagine how they'd explain the same topic to a 10-year-old schoolgirl and to an economics graduate. Would they use the same language? The same pictures? The lesson is of course that it's impossible to write and design in a way that communicates equally with everyone. Once you put pen to paper, you inevitably use a style that will appeal to some people more than others. The same goes for your website. Personas are therefore about playing to your strengths. Rather than trying to appeal to everyone and ending up pleasing no one, you choose the right customers and talk to them in their language.

However good your personas, don't let them become a safety blanket. They provide an ideal snapshot of users, but you should continually keep your knowledge fresh by talking with users and testing your designs.

SCENARIOS

Personas are useful tools to understand users, but they don't offer much insight into how people will interact with the site. You can use scenarios to explain why personas come to the site and how they use it to meet their goals.

Good scenarios tell the whole story of how the persona's problem is solved before, during, and after their interactions with your site. What tasks are they trying to achieve, and what needs do they have? How would they get to your site? Once they're on the site, where do they go? At what stages do they need to pause to gather information, review their options, or discuss with a friend? Does the story end happily ever after? Will they use the service again?

STORYBOARDS & COMICS

Scenarios are usually textual, but they're natural candidates for visual presentation. If you have time and confidence in your drawing ability, storyboards and comics can bring scenarios to life ⊞. All you need are some basic drawing skills—how to combine simple shapes into scenes and how to put people into basic poses—to make convincing stories. Just like a scenario, your storyboards can focus on details of users' lives, not just their limited interactions with the site.

H *Comics can communicate the context of a user's visit.*

We'll cover some basic sketching techniques in the next chapter, but if you're not confident in your abilities, you can create comics by taking posed photographs and tracing over them. There's plenty of software (such as Plasq's Comic Life, www.plasq.com/comiclife) to help you create convincing comics from scratch.

OTHER FORMATS

There are a few other well-known UX research deliverables—tools like Mental Models, popularized by Indi Young, and concept maps—but they're not ideal for undercover work. Instead, they excel on large projects that involve modeling an entire domain and very diverse user needs.

However, don't be afraid to improvise. You'll want your organization to see UX as a new, refreshing way to look at the world: is another dreary document going to excite your colleagues? Novel formats can be catalysts for conversation. Storyboards and comics are particularly unusual in business, but feel free to get creative and create your own formats. How about a newspaper-style report, or a small deck of persona playing cards?

Whatever the format, good research generates discussion. Your stakeholders or clients will want to contribute their own views on users and their tasks, and often these sessions will lead to conversations about possible design solutions. Next, we'll talk about how to take the hard work you've done in the discovery phase and generate ideas that put users first.

DISCOVERY: FURTHER READING

- *Observing the User Experience: A Practitioner's Guide to User Research*, by Mike Kuniavsky (Morgan Kaufmann, 2003)

- *Designing for the Digital Age: How to Create Human-Centered Products and Services*, by Kim Goodwin (Wiley, 2009)

- *The Inmates Are Running the Asylum: Why High-Tech Products Drive Us Crazy and How to Restore the Sanity*, by Alan Cooper (Sams, 1999)

- *Communicating Design: Developing Web Site Documentation for Design and Planning*, by Dan Brown (New Riders, 2010)

- *A Project Guide to UX Design: For User Experience Designers in the Field or in the Making*, by Russ Ungur and Carolyn Chandler (New Riders, 2009)

- *Information Architecture: Blueprints for the Web, 2nd Edition*, by Christina Wodtke and Austin Govella (New Riders, 2009)

- *Content Strategy for the Web*, by Kristina Halvorson (New Riders, 2009)

- *Unfolding the Napkin: The Hands-On Method for Solving Complex Problems with Simple Pictures*, by Dan Roam (Portfolio, 2009)

- *The Essential Persona Lifecycle: Your Guide to Building and Using Personas*, by Tamara Adlin and John Pruitt (Morgan Kaufmann, 2010)

- *The User Is Always Right: A Practical Guide to Creating and Using Personas for the Web*, by Steve Mulder with Ziv Yaar (New Riders, 2007)

- *Mental Models: Aligning Design Strategy with Human Behavior*, by Indi Young (Rosenfeld Media, 2008)

- *Card Sorting: Designing Usable Categories*, by Donna Spencer (Rosenfeld Media, 2009)

3

GENERATING IDEAS

After the hard work of research and analysis, finally you understand the design problem—or at least come close. Perhaps you even had your first glimpse of a solution. Buoyed with excitement or, more realistically, pressured by deadlines, it's tempting to kid yourself that you've experienced that breakthrough moment—a design epiphany. In reality, that first glimpse was more likely mirage than miracle. However exhilarating your first idea feels, it won't be your best.

Armed with the knowledge from your discovery phase, it's time to explore the world of ideas, looking for creative ways to design a great user experience. Generating ideas is enjoyable; the trick is to channel that energy in the right direction.

DIVERGENT THINKING

The key to generating a wide range of ideas is to think "divergently." If you've ever taken part in a brainstorming exercise, you'll recognize this way of thinking. Divergent thinking is broad and shallow, concerned more with quantity than quality. It suppresses the urge to appraise an idea, instead using each thought as a springboard to reach other ideas. With divergent thinking there are no bad ideas and no criticism. Smart answers are useful, but insightful questions are even better.

Divergent thinking comes naturally to some, but it can feel counterintuitive and unnatural when the pressure to find a solution is on. Fortunately, divergent thinking is a skill that can be learned like any other.

For best results, involve others. Divergent thinking isn't just for UX designers. Everyone sees from a different viewpoint, so use this to your advantage and work with your colleagues to generate ideas. You can be sure that others will see something you haven't, whether their ideas come from a short chat, a formal peer review, or a long collaborative design workshop (see the section "Collaborative Design," later in this chapter).

At this conceptual stage of the project, the risks are low. Don't be afraid to express bold ideas, and encourage others to do the same. Try to remove the fear of failure or embarrassment by setting an example and encourage others to follow suit.

Give people the space and time to generate good ideas. Consider, for instance, the physical space you work in. Moving away from the everyday office environment can generate excitement and get people thinking in new and interesting ways.

Autonomy and freedom usually motivate people, and creativity tends to evaporate if people feel constrained. Just be sure the open-ended nature of idea generation isn't seen as an excuse to drift. Stay focused on the problem you're trying to solve and stay within its boundaries.

★ SKETCHING

The undercover UX designer needs a quick and efficient way to describe dozens of ideas. Enter sketching.

Sketching has a low barrier to entry. Anyone can draw a line, and everyone has the requisite tools. Look around right now and you can probably lay your hands on something to draw with—no need for expensive software, batteries, or Wi-Fi.

Pen and paper sketches let you capture and revise ideas more quickly than any digital tool. They help you set your ideas free, rather than getting bogged down in detail. Sketches are unresolved, and abstract. They contain holes for ideas to grow into, and invite comment.

Sketches are expendable. Often, you'll discuss them once and then move on. It's a liberating feeling to know from the outset that you'll throw away most of your sketches. Suddenly you have the freedom to express any ideas, even the eccentric notions that won't stop whispering, "There's something in this."

Let's be honest: sketching is also good fun. Your job is to draw pictures for a living—tell your kids! Enjoyable work makes for a happier working environment and more motivation to succeed.

HOW TO SKETCH

People often respond to the notion of sketching with trepidation: "But I can't draw!" Let's kill this misconception now. In the words of graphic designer Jason Santa Maria, "Sketchbooks are not about being a good artist, they're about being a good thinker." You should use sketches to capture ideas, not demonstrate virtuosity, and with practice your skills will improve.

Different types of sketch fulfill different purposes for different audiences. UX design sketches usually fall into one of three modes.

Sketching for yourself

At one end of the scale, sketching is a visual way to capture your thoughts, for your eyes only **A**.

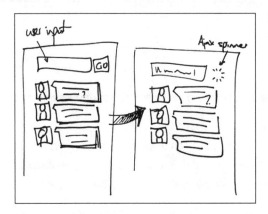

A Scribble down any ideas that you have, and don't worry about whether they're well drawn.

Your research will fill your brain with ideas; finally you have the opportunity to get them out of your head and into the world. Grab a pen and let your ideas flow onto the page. Don't worry if this outpouring of ideas leads to untidy sketches. Remember that you're going broad and shallow, not narrow and deep. The number and breadth of these sketches is more important than their artistic quality and legibility, and since these sketches are just for you, your audience is easy to please.

Visual communication

Communicating ideas to others requires a little more care than sketching for yourself. Whether it's the famous "back of the napkin" scribble to make a conversational point, or a group discussion around a whiteboard, your aim is to combine visual representation with discussion **B**.

These sketches exist purely to facilitate discussion, so they needn't be detailed, but they should at least be legible to others. The temporary nature of a whiteboard is perfect for this ephemeral approach.

B *Whiteboards are perfect for sharing ideas and provoking debate.*

Detailed sketching

As you explore the specifics of your designs, you can use a more precise sketch **C** to capture fine-grained details.

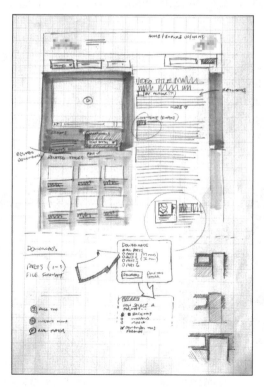

C *A detailed sketch encourages discussion of the finer details.*

Use a sketch if your thoughts are still divergent—that is, if you're provoking rather than resolving. If your thinking is more concrete you may prefer to create a more formal deliverable (see Chapter 4, "Making It Real").

TOOLS

It pays to have the right tools for the job. Take this as official clearance to visit the art supply store and stock up.

Canvas

When choosing sketching materials, pick convenience over quality. A pocket-size paper sketchbook will prove indispensable for visual note-taking and supporting impromptu design conversations.

A whiteboard or easel pad is more appropriate for groups. Even Picasso would struggle to use it elegantly, but that's not a problem. Gather your team around it when you need to solve problems collaboratively. Remember, standing up means no drawn-out meetings.

Pens

Fat-tip markers are ideal for exploring ideas **D**. Markers are cheap, durable, and easy to use. Their heavy line weight can be clumsy, but that's exactly what you want at this stage. You shouldn't be precious about your early sketches, and you don't want detail at the start.

D A small collection of pens will help you sketch better. Don't spend a fortune, but find tools you're comfortable with.

Later, as you begin to refine your ideas, you'll need tools with more precision. A set of fine-liner pens will be invaluable, but there's no need to go crazy.

Three weights—say 0.1mm, 0.5mm, and 1mm—will give the detail required for UX sketches.

For a touch of professionalism, buy a set of chisel-tip blendable gray markers. These markers are ideal for shading and shadows, which add extra visual appeal to your sketches.

TECHNIQUES

To describe digital interactions you'll deal mostly in two dimensions, so you needn't worry much about depth or perspective. Most UX sketches use just a few basic techniques and components; master these and you'll be an accomplished sketcher in no time.

Posture

Before you draw, adjust your posture. If you're tense and unbalanced, your sketch will be too. Try to relax and rest your non-drawing arm on the paper, so it won't slip around.

Lines and shapes

The humble line **E** forms the basis for almost everything you'll draw. It pays to get it right.

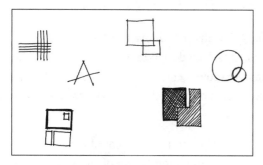

E *Lines and simple shapes are the fundamental units of sketching.*

Draw lines with intent and conviction. Delicate, feeble lines create fragile, unconvincing sketches. Use a single, controlled, fluid motion, rather than constructing a line with short overlapping segments. Give your lines an extra sense of purpose by adding a slight emphasis to their endpoints. To add further emphasis, simply double or triple the line.

When making basic shapes, let your lines overlap slightly where they meet. Unnecessary gaps make your sketch less solid.

Circles and ovals are tricky, but get easier with practice. Keep your wrist firm and rehearse the motion with the pen off the page first and you'll produce surprisingly even results.

Shadows and texture

If you're designing solely for a two-dimensional screen you may have little need for shadows or texture. However, any time you're working in three dimensions—for instance, creating a storyboard involving a tablet computer—shadows and texture ▫ can add surprising life to your sketches.

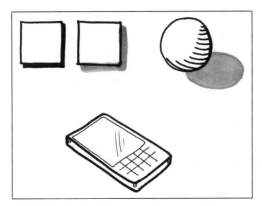

▫ *The two squares have simple drop shadows, while the sphere is drawn with both a cast shadow and a form shadow. The front of the cellphone is drawn with a glassy texture.*

There are three types of shadow. The **drop shadow** helps an image "float" above the page. It is often used in interface design to make elements such as buttons more prominent. The **cast shadow** is created by a solid object blocking light. It falls over the surface the object rests on, anchoring it. The **form shadow** is seen on the dark side of the object itself.

Conventionally, drop shadows appear below and to the right of objects, representing a light source emanating from the top-left corner of the screen. Drop shadows should be sharp and well defined. Cast shadows and form shadows vary depending on the position of the light source. Cast shadows can be softer when the light source is diffuse, and form shadows are softer still and follow the contours of the object.

Use your gray marker or hatched lines to add shadow. Take your time, take note of the shape of the object, and don't overdo it. Use an improvised real-life model for guidance if required.

Textures can be useful when sketching physical surfaces. Add a couple of sheen lines to represent glass, grain marks for wood, and so on.

Complex shapes and people

Complex shapes are usually just combinations of basic shapes. The key is to start with the largest elements. Draw the outline of a scrollbar before the arrows **G**, and draw the flank and neck of a giraffe before the head **H**.

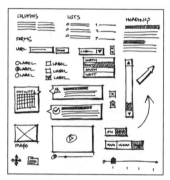

G *User interface controls are simply combinations of basic shapes.*

H *The same fundamentals, and a bit of practice, will help you draw more complex shapes and figures.*

Follow the same pattern to draw human figures. First sketch the torso, adding an angle if required to represent posture, then add limbs and work down to the smaller features. When you're confident using posture to represent context and emotion, you may wish to create figures using a single connected shape.

Heads should be approximately one seventh the height of the entire figure. Place eyes about halfway up the head and pay particular attention to eyebrows, which convey emotion surprisingly well. Point eyebrows inward to show anger, or askew to show confusion.

Don't worry about drawing detailed hands unless they're essential to the sketch. A curved box with the top half divided into four fingers will usually suffice. Extend a single rectangle to represent a finger.

Practice complex shapes by sketching everyday objects in your sketchbook. You'll soon develop an eye for the key features of an object.

Lettering

Legibility is your top priority when drawing letters ∎. Slow down and space the characters evenly. For short pieces of text such as annotations or dialogue, stick to uppercase for its consistency.

∎ *Take care with your lettering and aim for consistent size and weight.*

As with lines, try to emphasize the beginning and end of each stroke, and feel free to overlap lines slightly where they meet. Subtly angle the horizontal strokes of the letters upward to give them a more open feel.

For emphasis, add lines on either side of your original lines and, optionally, fill the spaces between them. For even stronger headings, create your letters with a gray marker and use a fine-liner to outline the characters.

If your letters will be contained within a speech bubble or thought bubble, write the text first and use a subtle drop shadow to lift the bubble off the page.

★ COLLABORATIVE DESIGN

As an undercover UX designer, you won't initially spend as long designing as you would like. Even if you did, you wouldn't have the authority to change whatever you please, since your stakeholders will have strong opinions about the site and how it should be developed. See this as a blessing, rather than a curse. By adopting a collaborative design approach, you can harness your colleagues' ideas and attack the problem more thoroughly and quickly than you could alone.

Collaborative design naturally encourages divergent thinking. Diverse stakeholders bring a broad range of perspectives, helping you to see the problem from many angles in a short timescale. Collaborative design also builds relationships early in the project and gives stakeholders a deeper interest in the design process. Establishing lines of communication, agreeing on goals and sharing understanding helps to avoid the them-and-us mentality that can result when design is conducted behind closed doors.

LEARNING TO LET GO

For all its benefits, collaborative design can be a worrying prospect. Everyone has experienced the frustration of a good idea being progressively diluted by too many cooks. Is collaborative design just another term for "design by committee?"

As long as you retain control of the process, the answer is no. Collaborative design isn't just about working together; it's an opportunity to set the tone of the project. Lead collaborative design efforts and you will have the perfect opportunity to set the UX agenda. Explain at the outset that you want the group to focus on user needs, not just their own.

It takes courage to kick-start a collaborative design process. Be prepared for a few failures along the way. Some of your initiatives will fly, while others will flop, and it's likely that people will only let you take the helm of minor projects until you prove your worth. But get collaborative design right and you'll have an extremely effective tool to introduce undercover UX.

Undercover user experience and collaborative design may seem like strange bedfellows, but remember our manifesto. We don't want to hide the user experience work—we want to get people excited about it without noticing. Collaborative design gives stakeholders the opportunity to express their pent-up ideas, and gives you a chance to introduce the UX way of thinking. As an added bonus, you'll also learn more about team dynamics: who does what, what biases they bring, and where you fit into the group.

A quick way to involve stakeholders in generating ideas is to hold a collaborative design workshop, in which you explain the problem and your research, and work together to explore dozens of possible solutions.

PLANNING A COLLABORATIVE DESIGN WORKSHOP

Before planning a collaborative design session, think about what you want from the session. Do you want ideas, debate, or consensus? Make sure you're clear on these high-level goals, so your workshop has focus.

Invite the right people

Invite a cross-section of your stakeholders, even if they're only likely to be heavily involved further down the line. Groups of more than 12 participants tend to become unmanageable, so you may need to hold more than one session.

Don't underestimate the logistical challenge of finding a suitable time slot in everyone's schedules. By all means emphasize the importance of the workshop and the urgency of fixing the UX issues on the site, but if you have time to spare it's generally better to wait for a time slot that everyone can make.

Practice

Schedule time in advance to get everything set. Prepare a summary of your research and select the exercises you'd like to run (see "Design games" below for some ideas). If you're covering unfamiliar territory, try out a cut-down version with close colleagues first. Until you become confident running collaborative design workshops, start with shorter sessions and smaller design challenges.

Get the right equipment

Provide every participant with same type of pen, preferably a fat-tip marker. This may sound pedantic, but it's worthwhile. First, everyone starts the exercise with the same equipment. It means everyone's designs can be treated equally and, when stuck on a wall, no one's work stands out more. Second, the quick and friendly nature of a marker is perfect for the rapid, high-level ideas we want to capture. Third, a fat marker line makes any photos you take of the sketches clear and easy to read. Avoid fine-liners and especially pencils, which are difficult to read from afar and don't show up well in photos.

Invest in good-quality sticky notes, so people's work won't fall down halfway through the session. Make sure everyone has the same size and colors of sticky note at their disposal. The standard yellow works well, but some exercises need extra colors. Book a room that has plenty of free wall space, and check that sticky notes actually stay stuck to its walls. Bring some masking tape for sticking up sketches, but first check to make sure it won't mark the wall.

> **TIP**
> Use a sharp downward movement to remove a sticky note from the pad. This prevents it from curling up when you stick it on the wall.

Bring plenty of blank paper for people to scrawl on, and any special paper your exercises require. You'll end up with a lot of sketches across dozens of sheets, so bring a decent digital camera to photograph the output.

Finally, a projector can be helpful when explaining your research, introducing an exercise or displaying the rules of a game.

RUNNING A COLLABORATIVE DESIGN WORKSHOP

Like public speaking, running a workshop involves a degree of performance. Participants will look to you to take the lead, so you want to be self-assured and help everyone feel at ease. Some of the exercises will take people away from their comfort zones, so plan to offer guidance and encouragement throughout the session. Avoid taking part in exercises yourself, so you can be on hand to help your participants.

Set the scene
Reiterate the goals of the workshop at the beginning. Emphasize that you are not necessarily looking for answers, just ideas, and that the short, playful exercises you'll go through are great ways to spark creativity. By reinforcing simple

notions like "there are no wrong answers" and "quantity not quality," you'll help reduce people's inhibitions.

Be a good host

Workshops can be hard work, so make sure people are comfortable throughout. Provide drinks, take regular breaks and, if you're running a longer workshop, be aware that people will tire toward the end of the day.

DESIGN GAMES

Design games are a perfect vehicle for collaborative design. Their hands-on, inclusive nature puts design in everyone's hands, encouraging a sense of shared ownership that other approaches lack. The communal spirit of adventure can break down barriers between team members and promote stronger team bonds.

Well-run games are enjoyable and memorable. People who are having fun tend to be more open to the unbounded nature of divergent thinking. Contrast this to a long requirements-gathering meeting—where would you rather be? This open thinking, spurred on by free conversation and creative activity, can reveal previously unspoken expectations. Remember the objectives, requirements, and unrequirements from the previous chapter? It's not unusual to find collaborative design exercises adding to or changing these lists.

However, games also come with baggage. Some stakeholders may not see the prospect of the team playing games as an appropriate use of time and money. In these circumstances, substitute a different label—try *exercise* if in doubt.

Here are some of the design games we use on a regular basis. Feel free to invent your own, or consult Donna Spencer's list at www.designgames.com.au for more inspiration.

Design the Box

The Design the Box game ◼ encourages participants to consider the product from the user's perspective. What do users need and want from the site? How can the site communicate with them? What will get them excited? It's an excellent icebreaker, and works well as the first exercise of a workshop.

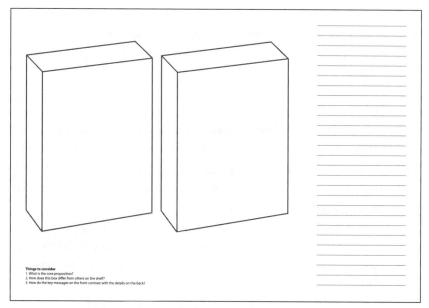

Things to consider
1. What is the core proposition?
2. How does this box differ from others on the shelf?
3. How do the key messages on the front contrast with the details on the back?

▌ *Design the Box focuses the team on what makes their product appeal to users. Download this template at www.undercoverux.com/resources.*

Divide people into small groups of three or four and ask each group to design and draw the packaging for the website, as if it were for sale on supermarket shelves. Ask them to think about the core proposition of the site and how to distil that down into a clear and concise form. Why would a customer choose this box over those next to it? What are the main messages the packaging should convey—perhaps the name, tagline and key features—and what details should be included on the reverse? Would the box include pictures or just text?

Allow plenty of time for this exercise, between 20 and 30 minutes depending on the size of the groups. At the end of the design phase, ask each group to stick their sketches on the walls, and discuss their ideas with the other participants.

Design the Box is an ideal way to open a discussion about what the site should do, how it stands out, and what it offers users. It forces people to think clearly about how the site—and the organization—must differentiate itself from competitors, and what features will appeal most to potential users. Participants must also consider the product's tone of voice, and key visual elements like color and imagery.

For an even more hands-on approach to Design the Box, provide a foldable card template, scissors, glue and colored pens so that your participants can make the box itself. You can then spread the various boxes around the office to spark further discussion.

The KJ Method

The KJ Method **K**, named after its Japanese creator Jiro Kawakita, helps groups reach consensus on what the most important aspects of a product should be. A single session using the KJ Method will generate dozens of ideas about user needs, features, grouping, and priority, which will directly guide your UX design work. Through a democratic process involving a wide cross-section of the organization, you encourage creativity while avoiding the dominant personalities or politics that so often hamper traditional meetings. The exercise lasts around an hour, so you can run it as a single meeting or slot it alongside other exercises in a longer workshop.

K *The KJ Method is a fast way to understand the group's thoughts about features and priority.*

First, establish a focus question, such as "What will users want to achieve when they visit this section of the site?" Spend some time sharpening this question; it's important to get it right.

Ask participants to work individually and think of as many answers as possible to the focus question, writing each one on a sticky note (make sure everyone is using the same color). Stop your participants after ten minutes, and ask them to put their sticky notes—in random order—on the wall.

Now, instruct participants to work together to group all of the sticky notes, by identifying similar items and clustering them on a separate part of the wall. Ask your participants to remain silent, but reassure them that they'll have the opportunity to discuss the exercise shortly. Some groupings will be easy if several people have put up similar notes, while some will be more contentious. Expect some silent disagreement and compromise in this communal exercise, and only stop when everyone seems happy with the final groupings.

The next task is to name the groups. Give participants some sticky notes of a new color and ask them to write down a name for each group that's been formed. If they want to further rearrange the groups to make the task easier, that's fine. To avoid the effects of groupthink, ask participants to keep their labels to themselves and again stay silent. Once everyone has written a name for each group, ask participants to stick their labels next to the corresponding groups.

At this stage you can pause for discussion or press on with the final task of voting. Ask participants to decide which three groups are the most important, in order of priority. Give everyone three final sticky notes in a third color, and ask them to draw three stars on the first, two on the second, and one on the last. Finally, ask participants to place these stars alongside their chosen groups, with their highest-priority group receiving three stars; the next group, two; and the lowest-priority group, one. Add up the votes to find the group's aggregate opinion on where the priorities lie.

By now, most groups will be desperate to discuss the exercise, so finish with a conversation about the answers, groups, labels, and priorities proposed.

Mobilify

Since any screen can be designed in thousands of ways, knowing where to start can be a headache. The Mobilify game helps you overcome the fear of the blank page by imposing the artificial constraint of a mobile device. Participants are asked to decide the order of page elements as seen on a rudimentary cellphone that can only display web pages vertically, from top to bottom.

Arrange participants into groups of two to four people, and ask them first to think of elements that could make up the web page in question. These can range from trivial elements such as a help link to complex components such as a registration form or a video clip. Ask participants to write each item on a sticky note and, if they have an opinion on how the element might look, to squeeze in a basic sketch. Finally, ask participants to stick their notes on the wall and, as a group, agree which elements are necessary and arrange them in the order they should appear on our hypothetical cellphone.

Mobilify forces participants to discuss what the most important things on the page really are, but the real value comes in the debate that typically ensues. People often begin the exercise with different preconceptions of the contents of each element, but in focusing on priority and form, the group must consider exactly what each element should be. You should emerge with a clearer picture of not only what makes up the page, but also how it should be arranged.

Design Consequences

Created by independent UX consultant Leisa Reichelt (www.disambiguity.com), the Design Consequences game generates multiple interface ideas and healthy discussion in a playful and engaging format. The slightly tweaked version below gives a simple form of rapid interface sketching an interesting twist that makes it particularly suitable for sites with longer user journeys.

Divide participants into groups of five or six. Tell each participant to pick a page or relevant area of the site, and give them five minutes to sketch a design for this page. Some participants will find this freedom daunting, so again clarify that you're not worried about neat drawing, just getting an idea down on paper.

Once the five minutes are up, ask everyone to briefly describe their sketch to the rest of their group, and allow five more minutes for the group to comment on any notable similarities or glaring differences. Provide some sticky notes for the group to record any salient points.

Now for the twist. Get each participant to pass his sketch to the person on his left. Ask participants to think about how they would interact with the interface they've been given—perhaps they'd push a button or click a link—and then sketch the next screen that they'd expect to see. They may choose to take ideas from the sketch they've been given, stick with the style of their original sketch, or create a sketch that combines the best parts of both designs.

After five more minutes, again ask participants to share their sketches with the group, describing the sketch they received, which screen they decided to draw next, and the features of their second design.

Using Design Consequences, a group can produce a wide array of ideas in a very short time. The range of perspectives can be eye-opening, and the page choices people make often reveal valuable information about perceived importance. The group will usually lean toward designing the screens it believes are the most important.

Six-to-One

Six-to-One, our version of an exercise popularized by Leah Buley and Brandon Schauer of Adaptive Path, also uses sketching to explore ideas rapidly.

Give each participant a "six-up" template of six basic grids ■, and ask everyone to produce six interface sketches within a fixed time frame—10 to 15 minutes should do it.

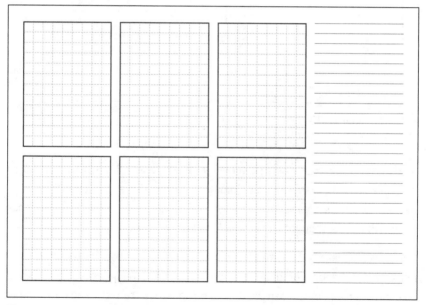

■ A "six-up" template encourages participants to squeeze out more ideas than they think they're capable of. Download this template at www.undercoverux.com/resources.

Once time runs out, ask participants to switch to a "one-up" template . They must now take their best ideas from the six-up phase and distill these into a single sketch, within the same time limit as before. The larger template encourages more detail, meaning participants must resolve some of the unanswered questions from their six-up sketches.

M *A "one-up" template lets participants explore their best ideas in more detail. Download this template at www.undercoverux.com/resources.*

At the end, stick everyone's sketches on a wall, and ask each participant to explain her ideas, warts and all. Comment on the similarities and differences between people's approaches, and ask the group to agree which approaches are worth further thought and which don't warrant further exploration.

The power of Six-to-One comes from forcing people to consider alternative solutions. The first couple of ideas come easily and are usually conservative, based on known conventions. When the tank of obvious ideas runs dry and participants have to think about different ways to tackle the design, the divergent thinking truly begins. Ideas emerge that would never otherwise be considered, and in turn spark new areas of inquiry.

Creative prompts

Although divergent thinking becomes more comfortable with practice, your participants may initially struggle to look from multiple viewpoints. To help ease the transition, consider using creative prompts that encourage people to think in new directions and conjure up interesting solutions.

One of the simplest forms of creative prompt is a prepared list of phrases such as "rotate", "sharing", and "images." Make your own list—it's much more enjoyable than using someone else's—and use these words as inspirational triggers. Other creative prompts include outputs from your research (personas or competitive analysis, for instance) or a scrapbook of visual ideas; even something as simple as screenshots and photographs on a shared drive. These stimuli can bring two apparently unrelated ideas together to suggest a new avenue of exploration. In the words of designer Alan Fletcher, sometimes one plus one can make three.

Should you want a more structured approach, consider how you would design a system for various user types. How would your site look if every user were a first time visitor? Or a regular customer? How would you design a screen that suits an impulsive shopper? Or someone who prefers to make decisions based on data?

If you're still making slow progress, try changing the scale at which you view the problem. Break the problem down into smaller components and tackle those first, or zoom out to see the problem from afar. For instance, could the problem be better solved elsewhere on the site? Or even elsewhere within the business?

Finally, you can provoke new ideas using custom-made tools like Stephen P Anderson's Mental Notes (www.getmentalnotes.com) or Dan Lockton's Design with Intent Toolkit (www.danlockton.com/dwi). These tools give insight into the psychology of design and suggest ways of thinking that incorporate these psychological principles.

★ SHARING THE SPARK

After generating so many creative ideas, it's important to sustain the momentum. Try not to let the organization forget about the UX cause and slip back into its usual mindset.

To keep the fire alive, share your sketches and the outputs of your collaborative design workshops. In particular, stick them up around your workspace in prominent places that are visible to passersby. Sketches and other visual tools are a rare sight in most businesses, and people will usually be curious to know more. Ideally, your sketches will catch a colleague's eye and cause him to stop for a closer look. You then have the perfect opportunity to answer his questions and talk about the user experience focus you've adopted.

Although sharing early concepts can seem premature, the rough and ready nature of your sketches announces that the problem is still unresolved, encouraging others to share their opinions. You can even put up a sign asking people to air their thoughts on your work, or leave a pen nearby so colleagues can add their own ideas.

In this way, the UX design cause spreads across the business, open to anyone who takes an interest. As curator of the concepts, you'll become known as someone who cares about the design of the site and the experience of users, but you'll also gain a reputation for openness and honesty. Your ideas, successes and mistakes are there for all to see, and your pride in your work shines through.

Finally, there's a personal benefit to having your concepts within easy reach. As you work on further concepts or flesh out the details of a proposed solution, your sketches show the shape of both individual pages and the whole site. You can scan ideas quickly while understanding how your design should fit in with the pages that accompany it.

If you're stuck in an open-plan office without any wall space of your own, see whether you can use communal areas such as break rooms or meeting rooms. You'll only need a large notice board, a wall, or a window. Do whatever you can to get the team's sketches and designs in plain view, but if wall space is truly at a premium, capture them with a scanner or digital camera, and share them through your intranet, wiki or email system. Electronic systems are more easily overlooked, but it's still preferable to hoarding the sketches on your desk, where they'll quickly be forgotten.

SKETCHBOARDS

Design consultancy Adaptive Path developed the sketchboard  as a simple, portable way to display design work in progress.

Every sketchboard starts with the same recipe. Find a suitable wall space, grab a big roll of brown parcel paper and stick up as large a sheet as your space allows. This paper will act as your canvas. Make sure there's plenty of room in front of the wall, otherwise you'll end up clambering over your colleagues.

Using masking tape, stick relevant background information such as personas, storyboards, or requirements onto the left-hand side of your canvas. This supporting information will guide the design and help you check whether an approach is suitable.

With your background material grouped on the left, use the remaining space to explore, share, and iterate on site designs. You can create columns to represent particular screens or steps in the user journey, or keep things freeform.

A sketchboard is an excellent format for sharing sketches. It's portable—simply roll it up and take it away—and it groups together important ideas and supporting information. It acts as a central repository for the project's creative output, meaning you can make decisions quickly without needing to hunt for documents and drawings on people's desks.

For more on sketchboards, see:
http://www.adaptivepath.com/ideas/essays/archives/000863.php

N A sketchboard from our work with the UK's Channel 4 News team.

■ Make your design principles memorable. Don't be afraid of humor or controversy if it helps the principles gain traction.

Once you have composed and agreed on your design principles with stakeholders, share them widely. Print them on postcards or posters and stick them around the office. The more people know and remember the principles, the easier it will be to refer to them.

Now use the principles to inform and validate your everyday design decisions. Just as you use a persona to assess the likely appeal of features, use design principles to gauge how well these features support the agreed user experience. See "Real-world design decisions" below for examples of how we have used design principles to guide our work.

REAL-WORLD DESIGN DECISIONS

Here's how our design principles affected the projects they were created for.

■ **We're local, not national.** *This principle lent an extra local bias to our designs, and spurred us to create fine-grained navigation that let the user drill down to individual neighborhoods.*

■ **Keep the user in flow.** *We honored this principle by offering natural break points in the data entry process, minimizing the points at which users had to switch between keyboard and mouse, and mapping a single real-world paper form to a single page on the site.*

■ **Let the world's natural beauty speak for itself.** *This design principle caused us to use photography prominently on each key page and provide clear donation calls to action alongside these persuasive images.*

Good design principles last. They may even outlast your involvement in the project. But they will live even longer if you update them as the project evolves. Build time to validate the principles in your team's design reviews, and make sure they remain central to the project's UX strategy. In doing so, you'll have a better chance to create the cohesive, holistic experiences your users will appreciate.

GENERATING IDEAS: FURTHER READING

■ *How Designers Think: The Design Process Demystified (4th edition)*, by Bryan Lawson (Architectural Press 2005)

■ *The Art Of Looking Sideways*, by Alan Fletcher (Phaidon Press Ltd 2001)

■ *Gamestorming: A Playbook for Innovators, Rulebreakers, and Changemakers*, by Dave Gray, Sunni Brown, James Macanufo (O'Reilly Media 2010)

■ *The Back of the Napkin: Solving Problems and Selling Ideas with Pictures*, by Dan Roam (Marshall Cavendish 2009)

■ *Innovation Games: Creating Breakthrough Products and Services*, by Luke Hohmann (Addison Wesley 2006)

■ *Universal Principles of Design: 100 Ways to Enhance Usability, Influence Perception, Increase Appeal, Make Better Design Decisions, and Teach through Design*, by Jill Butler, Kritina Holden, and Will Lidwell (Rockport Publishers Inc. 2007)

■ *101 Things I Learned in Architecture School*, by Matthew Frederick (MIT Press 2007)

■ *Sketching User Experiences: Getting the Design Right and the Right Design*, by Bill Buxton (Morgan Kaufmann 2007)

4

MAKING IT REAL

However deeply you have investigated the problem and however many creative ideas you have produced, you've little to show for your time until you turn your work into something concrete.

It's time to make things real. Where objectives, requirements, and unrequirements previously took a backseat to exploration, you should now look carefully at which of your ideas meet both business and user needs.

It's natural to have a hunch about which ideas you want to pursue. Now you should combine these diverse concepts into a more definite form. You're moving toward a complete design by adding detail, but there's still room to change your mind and tweak your designs as you go.

THE ROLE OF DELIVERABLES

We don't like jargon, but sometimes we're stuck with it. The word *deliverable* has become part ofthe UX vocabulary—a way to describe the outputs that UX designers share with stakeholders.

Whether these outputs are personas, sitemaps, or wireframes, creating deliverables is a craft that demands practice and expertise in the tools of the trade. It's not surprising, then, that user experience designers are sometimes guilty of "fetishizing" deliverables, seeing their creation as the *raison d'être* of great UX design. To an extent, this attitude is understandable since designers are often judged on the quality of their deliverables. There's nothing wrong with aiming high, but remember that in our manifesto we pledged allegiance to delivery. Deliverables are a stop on the journey, not the end of the line.

The most important role of deliverables is to document your design choices. Deliverables play an important role in the success of the project, helping you to communicate key concepts and the project's direction. They also reduce project risk by recording decisions made throughout the process.

But deliverables are more than mere documentation. They're also useful design tools. Just as a visual designer uses graphics software to work up an idea into a full page mockup, the UX designer needs a medium for refining ideas. Particularly in the early stages of project, the act of creating the deliverable can be as valuable as the deliverable itself.

Wireframes, personas, sitemaps, and other deliverables are therefore living documents, steadily getting closer to the final design with time. Some organizations struggle with this suspended uncertainty, believing that if a design is on paper it's final. If you work for this kind of company, be careful not to let people fixate on early designs.

★ DESIGN DELIVERABLES

In Chapter 2 we discussed deliverables that capture research findings. Now we'll focus on deliverables that you can use to document your ongoing design work.

SITEMAP

A sitemap is a visual representation of a site's structure ◼. Usually arranged hierarchically, sitemaps indicate how content and information are organized and, consequently, how users will navigate the system. A sitemap documents the system as a whole, pulling back from interface specifics to look from a broader vantage point.

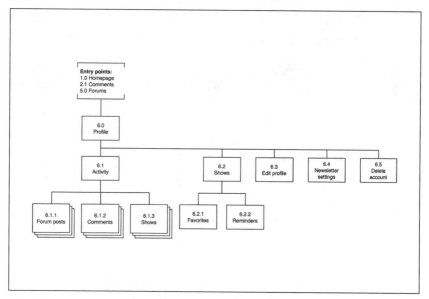

◼ This sitemap uses a top-to-bottom hierarchy to show site structure.

A sitemap is a familiar tool to every UX designer; you'll use one for most sites you design, particularly large, information-heavy sites. Use what you learned in your research (card sorts, interviews, and so on) to draft a structure that holds the site's content in a way that's meaningful to your users. It's worth starting this process as early as you can, so that you can fully appreciate the components of the system and what work lies ahead. It's not unusual to discover branches reaching farther than you expected.

Creating a sitemap will help you understand not only scope but also how sections and pages should be arranged and labeled. By the end of the exercise you should have a fair idea of how your site navigation will work, and what labels you should give to site sections.

Documenting a sitemap is a relatively simple task, thanks to Jesse James Garrett's visual vocabulary (www.jjg.net/ia/visvocab), in which you'll find a standardized set of shapes and connectors for use in your sitemaps and other deliverables. But don't let a sitemap's simplicity fool you: it will play an important role in the project. It might be the first deliverable you share with your team, so don't be surprised if it sparks debate. We'll talk more about feedback and critique in Chapter 5.

Since a sitemap is all about structure and hierarchy, starting with a text outline **B** can be useful. Tools like Microsoft Excel and the Omni Group's OmniOutliner will help you shuffle pages around before you start creating all those boxes and arrows.

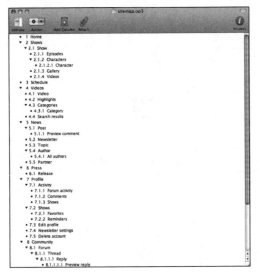

B *Text outlines help you plan the site's structure before you translate it into a visual sitemap.*

Sitemaps get big quickly, so make your drawing canvas as large as possible. Don't worry too much about laying the structure out beautifully; your sitemap will change a great deal over the course of the project. However, do try to use your software's connection tools properly, so that when you move a section, its connections move with it.

If your sitemap is becoming unwieldy, use the visual vocabulary's continuation-point symbol to break the sitemap into smaller subsections. Finally, add a simple numerical identifier to each page you depict. This will help you cross-reference pages with other deliverables.

USER FLOW

A user flow 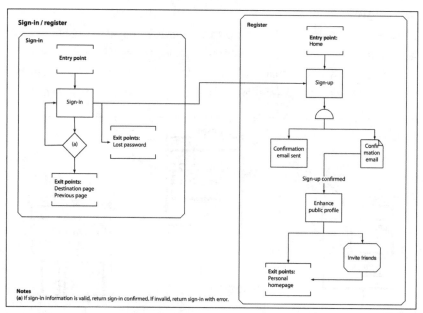 shows the steps a user can take to complete a task or activity.

C This user flow captures a sign-in/register process using Jesse James Garrett's visual vocabulary.

The simple hierarchical nature of a sitemap can be too limiting on sites with complex navigation, large amounts of user-generated content, or process-heavy applications that branch according to user input.

Under these circumstances a user flow may be more suitable. This deliverable describes how a user moves through a process, rather than capturing a hierarchical information structure. User flows are particularly suitable for task-driven sections of your site, such as creating a new account or adding an item to a shopping cart.

If only a few sections of your site are process-led, you can create a user flow in tandem with a sitemap; simply cross-reference the two using your numbering scheme.

User flows are great at explaining complex logic, but don't let them become swamped with detail. It's easy to overwhelm user flows with irrelevant minutiae. Instead, pay attention to the high-level interactions. You might also need to consult with your developers if your proposed solution involves tricky technical logic.

Wireflow

Like a user flow, a wireflow **D** shows how a user moves through the site, but replaces labels with rough representations of the relevant interfaces. Wireflows are particularly effective when the behavior of the interface is unconventional and demands visual explanation. Again, a wireflow and a sitemap can work well together.

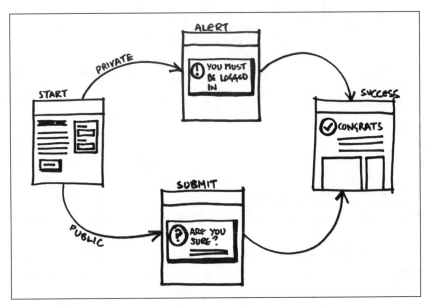

D This sketched wireflow combines high-level user flow with basic screen layout.

Storyboard

Storyboards **E** are another powerful tool for illustrating user flow. We covered storyboards as research deliverables in Chapter 2, but you can also use them at this stage to show how the interface behaves and any offline activity or thought processes required of the user.

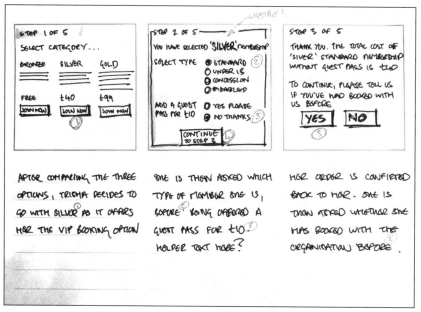

E Storyboards let you add instructional detail to complex interactions.

Scenarios, if created in your research phase, make excellent starting points for illustrating user journeys. You can show users in their context of use (home, office, and so on) and any interactions or emotional responses that take place off the screen.

Storyboards excel when an interaction is difficult to communicate using an abstract deliverable like a sitemap or user flow. A storyboard's visual and narrative approach gives an additional layer of context.

It's impractical to storyboard your entire site, but presented alongside other deliverables, storyboards can offer the extra level of detail required for crucial interactions.

To save time, use a single frame to show related interactions, labeled with numbers to show the order in which they occur. Thought and speech bubbles can be a useful adjunct to textual descriptions, adding character and helping to humanize the storyboard. Keep your output simple in case you want to start over.

TIP

Save time by using a storyboard template, available for free online:

- Konigi's OmniGraffle template (www.konigi.com/tools/omnigraffle-ux-template) and Graph Paper (www.konigi.com/tools/graph-paper)
- Comic book–style templates from the Sun.com customer experience team (http://blogs.sun.com/MartinHardee/entry/design_comics_templates_1_0)

WIREFRAME

A wireframe 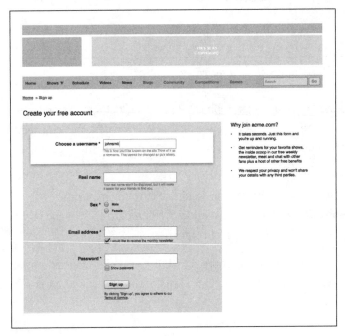 is a low-detail representation of an interface. It omits color, image detail, and other visual design specifics, providing instead a simple inventory of what's on the page and how it should be laid out.

F *This wireframe shows the first screen of a sign-up process.*

A wireframe addresses several design issues:

- Information organization. Which items should be grouped and where? Are there any particular relationships that need to be made more evident than others? How should these groups be prioritized?

- Content. What content needs to be present on the page? Will it be prose alone or does the page need to accommodate images and video?

- Functionality and controls. What can users do on the page? How will users navigate the site? Is there a search function? A log-in control? Are there any inputs such as forms?

- States. What are the various states of the page? How do forms handle errors? Does the page vary depending on the user's status—for example, logged in versus logged out?

- Behavior. Are there interactions that happen without a full page refresh? How does the page respond to input?

- Metadata. What page is this? How does it relate to the sitemap? What project does it belong to? Who is the author? What version is it?

- Annotation. Nuanced interactions or complex points may need further explanation. Use annotation callouts to highlight these areas.

> **NOTE**
>
> It can be hard to capture page behavior with static wireframes. If your design requires rich interaction, then storyboards or a prototype may be more suitable ways to explain site behavior.

The wireframe has long been the bread and butter of user experience design, and will undoubtedly be one of your most commonly made deliverables. With practice you should be able to produce a wireframe quickly, freeing up more time to discuss it with others and explain your design choices.

Try to ensure that your wireframes show consistency between pages; it can be easy to focus on an individual page and lose sight of how other pages are designed. If you are confident in your HTML skills, you may also want to include some suggestions about semantic markup on your wireframe, to help communicate its structure to your developer colleagues.

PAGE DESCRIPTION DIAGRAM

A page description diagram (PDD) **G** is a written inventory of every element on your web page. Elements are categorized into high, medium, and low priority and ordered horizontally.

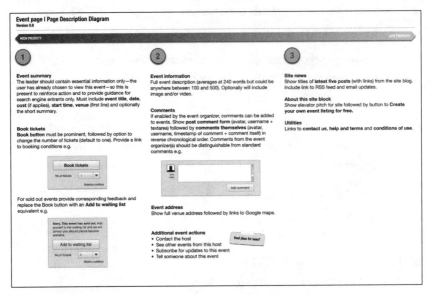

G *This page description diagram shows the contents of a page in priority order.*

Wireframes may be the most commonly used tool in the UX designer's kit, but they aren't always suitable. If visual or graphic designers are currently in charge of deciding layout—what goes where on the page—they may complain that your wireframe relegates them to the role of "coloring the boxes." A PDD might be a better approach in this scenario.

Dan Brown of EightShapes invented the PDD as a way for UX designers to explain content hierarchy without dictating the specifics of layout. The PDD describes what's important to a UX designer—the contents of the page and which are the most important for common user tasks—without stepping too far into the time-consuming world of layout.

PDDs leave the door open for visual designers to interpret page layout, while allowing stakeholders to focus on the important issues of content and priority. This makes PDDs ideal if you're trying to squeeze a user experience focus into an existing design process.

If an element within your PDD needs more visual detail, you can supplement its text description with a simple diagram.

PROTOTYPE

A prototype  is a simplified but functional model of a system, used to explore, communicate, and test a design. Users can move directly through a prototype, with pages following each other in chronological order.

H *An HTML prototype being used for usability testing.*

The previous deliverables are all in some way abstracted from the final product. Stakeholders must imagine how these documents will translate into a finished website. However, stakeholders who aren't familiar with user experience may not be convinced by skeletal deliverables. Instead, they will want to see solutions.

Prototypes excel at presenting solutions, since they involve the smallest leap of imagination between deliverable and end product. They let people experience the real flow of a system, meaning your stakeholders can feel firsthand the benefit of good user experience. It's better to test-drive a car than to look at it in the showroom.

An effective prototype will not only communicate your design to stakeholders, but also enthuse them in a way no other deliverable can. Get a senior manager excited by a prototype, and your battle to integrate UX is already half won.

Prototypes also have the great advantage that you can run usability tests with them. We'll cover that in the next chapter, but for now, get buy-in for the concept by explaining that a prototype allows you to gather insight into what works for real customers and what doesn't. Couple this with the message that a prototype will help you incorporate customer feedback before costs become too high, and you'll have a compelling argument for your case.

The most obvious downside of a prototype is the effort required. A prototype takes longer to build and calls for more specialized skill than other deliverables, and if your assumptions and decisions are wrong, you could waste time.

To minimize the time you spend on your prototype, remember that you're not looking to create the real thing. Don't worry about polish—quality of code, beautiful aesthetics—you're only after a platform to demonstrate and test your ideas. Rough edges are a necessary part of the bargain.

A prototype will typically change beyond recognition as the project progresses. Make it modular and disposable. It's not a good idea to use the code of a prototype as a basis for the actual website; you're more interested in making it work than making it perfect.

FUNCTIONAL SPECIFICATION

A functional specification ∎ is a detailed document describing in full the behavior of your site, its functionality, and how it responds to user input.

Due to the effort involved, the functional specification has fallen out of favor in modern web design. However, some organizations—such as those in high-risk sectors that employ a "waterfall" model where design fully precedes development—still embrace this deliverable.

A functional specification poses a headache to any user experience designer, particularly an undercover one. Once created, it demands that the design be locked down, since the work required to change it later is so great. As such, UX designers often dissuade their businesses from demanding a functional specification, and instead try to sell the benefits of testing and iteration.

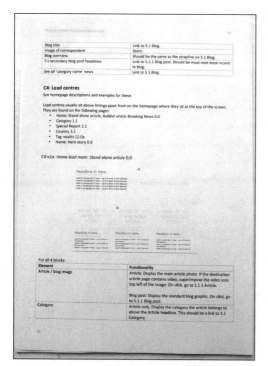

■ *This functional specification documents the design and functionality of a news website.*

If you have no other option than to create a functional specification, investigate whether this would be your responsibility or whether a product owner or business analyst might be able to generate one from a prototype. If the responsibility falls to you, set aside a lot of time and prepare for some painstaking work.

★ FIDELITY

The term *fidelity* describes the level of detail of your deliverables. *Low-fidelity* deliverables are a rough approximation of the intended user experience. They're quick and dirty, capturing the essential characteristics of the site. *High-fidelity* deliverables give a more accurate representation of the site, including not just core features but also specifics of the site's behavior and even aspects of the final visual design.

The right fidelity for your deliverables will depend on your project. Before talking about that decision, let's look at how fidelity affects the tools and techniques you use (and vice versa), and which fidelity is most suited to which deliverables.

LOW FIDELITY

Low-fidelity tools are increasingly popular in UX design. With no technical knowledge required, you can create lo-fi deliverables with very little fuss.

LOW-FIDELITY TOOLS

- *Paper. Save time by making printed templates containing boxes, browser windows, and so on.*

- *Pens. As before, fat-tip markers for broad strokes, fine-liners for detail.*

- *Scissors and sticky tape. For cutting up and recombining your paper components.*

- *Sticky notes, index cards, overhead-projector transparencies. To mimic interactions like pop-ups and dialog boxes.*

Pen and paper deliverables are extremely versatile: you can use them to produce almost any deliverable, from sitemaps to wireframes and even paper prototypes. Hand-drawn deliverables are very quick to produce and easy to improve upon, but production time will quickly mount up if you need to redraw the same elements over and over again.

Low-fidelity deliverables don't make for good formal documentation, but they're ideal when you need to convey decisions quickly. In Chapter 3 we explained how to use a detailed sketch to convey an idea; the hand-drawn wireframe ◫ uses the same techniques and tools but offers more detail, proposing a solution rather than exploring a concept. It includes annotations that explain the major components of the page and how they work together.

Paper prototypes ◰ are an easy way to test complex systems without the time and expense of making a digital prototype. Use sticky notes to represent panels that open and close, use overhead-projector transparencies for pop-up windows, and cut out your navigation and tape it to a background "master" so you don't have to recreate it on every page. Paper prototypes need someone "behind the scenes" to operate the system based on the actions of the user: opening drop-down menus, entering data, and so on.

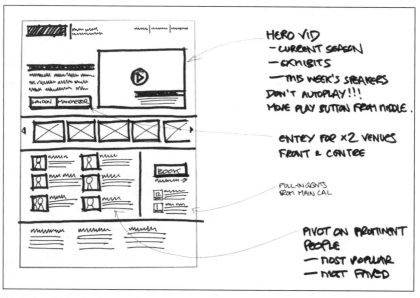

J *This low-fidelity wireframe, although hand-drawn, includes more detail than an exploratory sketch.*

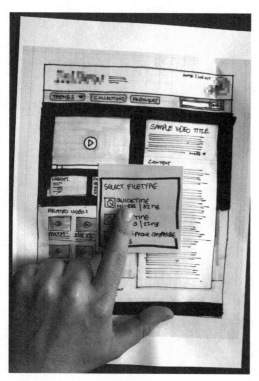

K *This paper prototype uses sticky notes to mimic user interaction.*

MEDIUM FIDELITY

When you need more detail than a sketch, it's time to pull out the professional tools. Although they demand more investment of time and money than a simple sketch, they provide professional output and the flexibility to make changes without having to redraw everything from scratch.

MEDIUM-FIDELITY TOOLS

- *The Omni Group OmniGraffle (for Mac, from $100; for iPad, $50; www.omnigroup.com/products/omnigraffle)*

- *Microsoft Visio (for PC, from $260; http://office.microsoft.com/en-us/visio)*

- *Adobe Fireworks (for PC or Mac, $299; www.adobe.com/products/fireworks)*

- *Adobe Illustrator (for PC or Mac, $599; www.adobe.com/products/illustrator)*

- *Apple Keynote (for Mac, $79; www.apple.com/iwork/keynote)*

- *Microsoft PowerPoint (for PC or Mac, $230; http://office.microsoft.com/en-us/powerpoint)*

- *Balsamiq Mockups (for PC or Mac, $79; www.balsamiq.com/products/mockups)*

- *Mockingbird (web-based, from $9/month; http://gomockingbird.com)*

- *HTML image maps. Clickable "hotspots" can be positioned over any image in a web browser—a simple way to add hyperlinks to flat graphics files.*

If you want to create a family of deliverables with shared elements, you'll immediately benefit from being able to copy and paste elements between documents. Many of these tools offer sophisticated functionality such as master layers and shared libraries, allowing you to create your own collection of templates and stencils to reuse across projects. If you're producing lots of deliverables, this efficiency alone is probably a good enough reason to adopt medium-fidelity tools.

Professional tools let you export to a wide range of formats including graphics files, PDF, and even HTML, making it easy to share your deliverables with stakeholders across the world.

The medium-fidelity wireframe 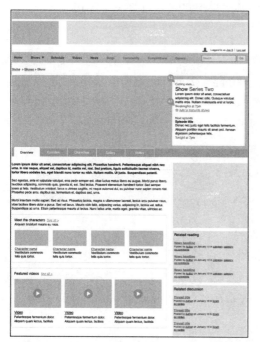, created using the Omni Group's OmniGraffle software, shows a page with placeholder images and annotations.

■ A medium-fidelity wireframe conveys more detail than its low-fidelity counterpart.

If you want to demonstrate basic interactivity, you can also use medium-fidelity tools to create simple clickable wireframes ■

■ Clickable wireframes let you mock up basic interactions such as adding an item to a shopping cart.

Presentation tools like Keynote and PowerPoint, although not specifically designed for creating design mockups, make this surprisingly easy. Keynote in particular has several built-in motion transitions that mimic the visual behavior of interactive web applications.

Dedicated tools like OmniGraffle, Visio, and Fireworks include basic prototyping features and can easily be extended with shared libraries and stencils.

HIGH FIDELITY

If your product includes particularly nuanced interactions, or you need to include significant visual detail, you should create high-fidelity deliverables. In the UX world, this high level of fidelity usually means creating a prototype.

HIGH-FIDELITY TOOLS

- *Adobe Dreamweaver (for PC or Mac, $399; www.adobe.com/products/ dreamweaver)*

- *Adobe Flash Professional (for PC or Mac, $699; www.adobe.com/ products/flash)*

- *Adobe Flash Catalyst (for PC or Mac, $399; www.adobe.com/products/ flashcatalyst)*

- *Axure (for PC or Mac, $589; www.axure.com)*

- *HTML, CSS, and JavaScript. There's little or no cost attached to using these technologies for prototypes—all you need is a text editor and a browser.*

Specialist prototyping tools such as Axure can reduce the steep learning curve often associated with high-fidelity prototyping. Like some of the medium-fidelity tools, these specialist tools provide a WYSIWYG interface and generate functional HTML to allow your prototype to run in a browser.

Alternatively, you can get your hands dirty with HTML, CSS, and JavaScript yourself . This can be daunting, but fortunately there are a number of libraries and frameworks that can reduce the legwork involved in layout, cross-browser compatibility, and interaction.

N *Screenshot showing a usability test conducted on a high-fidelity HTML prototype.*

NOTE

- Popular CSS frameworks include Blueprint (www.blueprintcss.org) and the 960 Grid System (www.960.gs).

- To prototype interactions, use JavaScript libraries such as jQuery (www.jquery. com) and MooTools (www.mootools.net). If you're not well versed in JavaScript, the IxEdit tool (www.ixedit.com) can help generate the code required.

- Basic PHP can be an excellent addition to your prototyping palette. PHP lets you reuse code efficiently across pages, and using basic string functions, you can mock up surprisingly complex search components.

CHOOSING FIDELITY

A useful principle for undercover work is to adopt the lowest fidelity necessary to get the job done. What you lose in detail you'll gain back in time and effort. However, the most appropriate level of fidelity for your deliverables will depend on several factors.

Audience

Your deliverables should be tailored for your stakeholders, so that you don't underdeliver or waste time that you could use elsewhere.

Stakeholders will have differing needs from your deliverables; specifically, they'll need enough information to do their jobs. For example, product owners will be eager to see whether solutions meet business objectives. Content specialists will want to know what copy needs to be created and where it should go. Developers will want to learn about required functionality.

In some instances, you'll be able to provide further detail and clear up ambiguity with a discussion. There's no point creating glossy deliverables for the person sitting next to you; sometimes, a simple picture and a conversation is all you need to get your message across.

Also consider what you learned in your cultural analysis of the organization. Some stakeholders will respond better to high-fidelity deliverables, whereas others will be happy with a sketch of the essentials.

You may be able to create a single deliverable that covers these diverse needs, or you may need to create a couple of versions to explain relevant items in more detail. Just remember that extra deliverables take extra time to create and maintain.

Finally, if you plan to conduct usability testing with these deliverables, you should use a higher-fidelity method, although this will also depend on the goal of your testing. Medium-fidelity deliverables might suffice for simple tests of basic elements, but for subtle interactions or those that will depend on particular content, a high-fidelity prototype is ideal.

Time

As an undercover UX designer, it's better to work on the design than create beautiful deliverables. While this clearly implies that low fidelity is desirable, you must find the balance. Too much haste will lead to ambiguity or confusion, meaning wasted time revisiting your deliverables or clarifying the situation. If in doubt, use the tools with which you are most comfortable.

You can reduce time pressures if you can take advantage of other resources. Could you convince the business to let a willing developer convert your sketches into a high-fidelity prototype?

Life span

Most deliverables are made obsolete when the site goes live, but until that point remember that every deliverable you create will have to be kept up-to-date. This can be especially time-consuming if you're creating several types of deliverable.

Scope

How much of the site experience do your deliverables need to capture? A sitemap and handful of wireframes that capture a single user journey may provide enough detail for your team, or you may need to depict lots of journeys and permutations. Be careful not to overcommit. Let your scope and fidelity be guided by what you can realistically achieve.

Innie or outtie

Outties—external agency staff or consultants—typically have to produce higher-fidelity deliverables than innies. Deliverables will usually form part of an agency contract, and can be the only way for the client company to assess the quality of thought and work they are getting for their money.

Agencies may have agreed formats for deliverables; be sure to match these to reduce the risk of wasted work.

★ BETTER DELIVERABLES

There's no perfect way to make deliverables; the best approach depends on the project and your personal style. However, since an undercover designer's deliverables will be central to the case for UX, here are some tips on how to get the most out of them.

TRY EVERYTHING, MASTER SOMETHING

Try out various tools to develop your proficiency and appreciate which of them are best suited to which deliverables. Most of the software listed in this chapter has a free trial version, so get downloading and experimenting.

You'll probably find that one tool suits you better than the others, or perhaps you'll be limited to one application since that's all that your organization can offer. Take the time to learn the nuances of that tool and become a real expert in it. Keyboard shortcuts will save you hours, as will learning how to create master templates and stencil libraries.

The largest risk with this approach is that you'll fixate on your chosen tool as the only appropriate answer to every problem. Be sure to choose your weapon based on the problem at hand, not just on whatever's most comfortable.

CONSULT DESIGN PATTERN LIBRARIES

A pattern library **O** documents effective solutions to a common problem. Each pattern explains the problem, the proposed solution, and the context in which the problem occurs.

As users have become more familiar with the web, standardized approaches to targeted problems have begun to emerge. Pattern libraries document these designs, and detail the rationale behind them.

Design patterns won't make your design decisions for you, but they can be a shortcut past some of the legwork you'd otherwise have to do yourself. They can save you time and reinforce your decisions with the knowledge that others have successfully tested these approaches over the years.

O *Popular pattern libraries include Yahoo Pattern Library (http://developer.yahoo.com/ypatterns), Quince (http://quince.infragistics.com), and Martijn van Welie's collection (www.welie.com).*

However, be careful not to apply patterns blindly. A design that works elsewhere isn't guaranteed to work on your site, and a subtle difference in requirements can render an approach invalid.

BUILD A PERSONAL LIBRARY

As you gain experience, you'll inevitably build up a set of stencils, shapes, and templates that suits your style. By continually tweaking the set and making it your own, you'll end up with a set of tools that can act as your own artist's palette.

Similarly, you'll subconsciously build your own library of design patterns that work well for specific problems. Take the time to build these into a design pattern library of your own, and you'll find yourself becoming more efficient, focusing on your design rather than the tool you're using.

If you're on a team, share these stencils, templates, and design snippets on a shared drive or intranet. If you're prototyping in HTML, ask whether your developers have a library of code snippets that can save you coding time.

LEARN HTML AND CSS

While we're on the topic, since HTML and CSS are the media you work in, learn them. Just as a composer must know the range of each instrument she writes for, learning HTML and CSS will help you truly understand the possibilities and limitations of web technology.

The fundamentals are surprisingly simple and take only a couple of weeks to pick up. Don't worry about advanced tricks, but learn enough so that you would know how to start coding your wireframes. Not only will HTML and CSS give you another viable prototyping option, but also they will improve the quality of your designs and help you communicate better with your developer colleagues.

TIP
- There are dozens of online tutorials to help you learn HTML and CSS, such as www.w3schools.com; and books such as *Designing with Web Standards*, (*3rd edition*) by Jeffrey Zeldman (New Riders, 2009), which give an excellent grounding in modern standards-based web development.
- The WaSP InterAct curriculum can be a useful reference (http://interact. webstandards.org/curriculum/front-end-development).

IDENTIFY KEY PAGES

Each site has a couple of pages that lie at the heart of the user experience. For example, the photo-sharing site Flickr centers around just two key pages: the photo page and a user's photo stream. Without these, the hundreds of other pages on the site could not exist.

Make key pages your top priority since their structure and design will affect the rest of the site. You should already have a hunch about which pages are key—your sitemap and design principles will often help to highlight them. Give key pages the attention they deserve, and your site's user experience is off to a great start.

It's rare that the homepage is a key page. Although it's an irresistible draw for stakeholders, the homepage's main job is usually to direct visitors to the key pages. Designing a good homepage is easier once you've defined the core essence of the site; as such, consider leaving it until later.

GET THE MAIN FUNCTION RIGHT

Similar logic applies within a page. It's better to get a page's main function absolutely right and forget about the rest, than to spread your effort thinly. It's easy to lose sight of what really matters when your head's full of competing requirements. If you find yourself struggling, break the problem down. What is the one thing this page needs to accomplish? Forget the secondary content—sidebars, footers, and so on—and focus on the core.

EXPLORE AS YOU GO

Although you're starting to converge toward a final design, don't be afraid to explore new alternatives as they crop up. You can use any of the techniques discussed in Chapter 3.

The line between generating ideas and refining them is blurry. It's OK to switch between the two modes, although in later stages you should focus on polishing the details rather than generating additional ideas.

CONSIDER THE 'FIRST-RUN' EXPERIENCE

Pay special attention to the user's first experience with your site. Is the site clear about what it does and how it should be used? It's easy to neglect this state if you're short on time, but even though a user may only see this state once, the first experience forms the important first impression.

If you're designing a site that relies on user-generated content, remember to design the "blank slate": how the page will look without this content. A design that seems active and useful once it's full of content can appear imbalanced and deserted without that content. Provide direction and incentives for users to contribute so that the site's emptiness doesn't appear intimidating.

USE REAL CONTENT

For years, UX designers created wireframes and prototypes with "lorem ipsum," dummy text indicating that the real content would follow later.

Designing around dummy text means that you have no way of knowing if the main visual focus of the page matches the main written focus of the page. Without knowing what's on the page, you may leave too much space, or too little. Dummy text also means you can't run valid usability tests on the system, since real users will want to read the text and look for trigger words.

Use real content wherever possible. If the content is unavailable, outdated, or being rewritten, talk with your content providers about the contents of the page, what its features are, how long it is, and what the main focus and calls to action should be.

> **NOTE**
>
> If you must use lorem ipsum, online tools such as www.lorem2.com can generate the text for you in a variety of formats.

As an undercover designer, you may have to use lorem ipsum if you don't have access to content providers. However, aim to replace it with real content—even a first draft—as soon as you're able. Only then will you be able to judge whether the design and content together meet your users' goals.

COME UP FOR AIR

Creating deliverables can be enjoyable, but be careful not to drown in detail.

A simple and effective way to avoid losing focus is to build regular peer review into your routine. We'll cover formal critique in the next chapter, but before that point, consider whether you can share work in progress with close coworkers who are sympathetic to the UX cause. This could be something as simple as an impromptu discussion: simply print out your designs and take them to your colleagues for their thoughts. If you find yourself stuck on a problem, a few minutes spent describing it to colleagues can force you to focus on the heart of the issue.

A more advanced form of peer review is pair design, where you and a colleague work on a design simultaneously at one desk. Pair programming, the developer equivalent, is common within Agile environments (see Chapter 6, "Working with..."), where it's used to improve quality and create easily maintainable code. Applying the same technique to UX design can drive up the quality of your work and help colleagues buy in to your recommendations.

Although it's common for UX designers to conduct pair design together, you can partner with anyone involved in the project: developers, visual designers, content specialists, and so on. If you're using software while pair designing, let one person "drive," sitting at the computer, while the other provides input and suggestions. Swap every hour or so to keep things fresh.

Of course, pair design takes two people, so it can be tricky to arrange. However, it will teach you a great deal and can help build strong relationships.

MAKING IT REAL: FURTHER READING

- *Web Anatomy: Interaction Design Frameworks that Work,*
  by Robert Hoekman, Jr. & Jared Spool (New Riders, 2010)

- *Prototyping: A Practitioner's Guide,* by Todd Zaki Warfel (Rosenfeld Media, 2009)

- *Search Patterns,* by Peter Morville & Jeffery Callender (O'Reilly Media, 2010)

- *A Project Guide to UX Design: For User Experience Designers in the Field or in the Making,* by Russ Unger and Carolyn Chandler (New Riders, 2009)

- *Web Form Design: Filling in the Blanks,* by Luke Wroblewski (Rosenfeld Media, 2008)

- *Designing Interfaces: Patterns for Effective Interaction Design,*
  by Jenifer Tidwell (O'Reilly Media, 2006)

- *Communicating Design: Developing Web Site Documentation for Design and Planning,* by Daniel M Brown (New Riders, 2007)

- *Information Architecture: Blueprints for the Web, 2nd Edition,*
  by Christina Wodtke and Austin Govella (New Riders, 2009)

5

REFINING YOUR SOLUTION

You've researched the problem and learned about your users. You've explored several designs and documented the best of them. Now it's time to break from cover, get feedback from your stakeholders, test your ideas with users, and tweak your design.

In many business fields, revisiting old ground is an admission of failure—"Didn't we just do this bit?"—but design thrives on iteration. We've already discussed how your first design can never fully solve the problem, since it's impossible to uncover all objectives, requirements, and unrequirements in advance. Even if you could have a complete picture at the start of a project, circumstances change. Users adopt new online habits. Competitors reveal products that make yours obsolete. New technology makes the previously impossible run-of-the-mill.

You never know that a design is successful until it's being used. The site could meet your business requirements exactly but be hated by users, or give users exactly what they want while making the company lose money. Even successful designs create problems. Increasing sales on your website by 50 percent is fantastic, until your shipping channels are overwhelmed and deliveries are slow. You then face the new design challenge of managing users' expectations about delivery dates. Design is a never-ending mission.

★ THE NATURE OF ITERATION

Iteration can occur on any scale, from revising the entire site's information architecture, to tweaking the layout of a single page. Usually you'll be updating the deliverables you created in Chapter 4, although sometimes you'll want to go back to consider additional research and new ideas. Iteration is about sharpening your design by throwing out ideas that have outlasted their shelf life, and replacing them with fresh ones. If it's broke, fix it.

The web is especially well suited to iteration. Pioneers of the web thrive on the freedom of adapting code, trying new approaches, and testing the limits of the browser and the user. By contrast, designers who work in more tangible media are under enormous pressure to get things right first time. The consequences of changing a website are relatively minor—wasted time and upset developers—compared with the disaster of changing architectural blueprints after half the bricks have been laid.

Don't underestimate the time iteration will take. Less experienced designers are often so sure their first design is The One that they don't allow enough time to gather solid feedback and make necessary changes. With time, these designers learn to approach matters differently. Instead of wanting to be proved right, good designers want to be proved wrong.

The fuel for iteration comes from two sources: stakeholders and users. Although the obvious route is to gather stakeholder feedback first, for undercover work we recommend running tests with users first, turning hypothesis into fact. Usability tests give you ammunition to support your design decisions along with insight into which approaches don't work. The more data you can bring to a stakeholder critique session, the better.

Holding usability tests before stakeholder critique may also encourage your colleagues to watch the tests for an early glimpse of the design. Not only does this help you sell the benefits of testing, but also stakeholders begin to appreciate issues from user perspectives as well as their own.

That said, it's not always possible to test a site with users unless stakeholders know what you're testing. Under these circumstances, you may need to hold a stakeholder review session first to get permission for tests (see "Critique," later in this chapter).

★ TESTING WITH USERS

UX designers know, of course, that user input is essential for iteration, but businesses aren't always so keen on it. Stakeholders often fear that usability testing will be slow and expensive. Thankfully, the days of labs and expensive equipment are gone. With nothing more than a laptop, cheap software, and a few spare hours, undercover usability tests will show you what you got right and what still needs work.

There are two general types of usability test. A **summative** test looks at an existing system, either as a prelaunch check or an analysis of a

> **NOTE**
> Stakeholders also often make the classic argument "The site makes sense to me!" It's easy to counter by pointing out that your colleague knows the site and subject matter in depth, and thus isn't representative of a real user.

site you'd like to improve. It can make for a great introductory exercise into UX, and forms the basis of the corridor test we discussed in Chapter 2. However, our main focus within the design process is on **formative** testing, conducted on an unfinished system to gain insight on how to improve the design.

User feedback sessions give you the opportunity not only to conduct formative tests, but also to expand your knowledge of users. If you didn't have much time to research in advance, try scheduling regular dual-purpose sessions throughout the project. Early in the project, use these sessions for extra research, then as you begin to generate designs to test, phase out research and phase in formative usability testing ▲. By the end of the project, when your design is nearly complete and you're confident in your knowledge of users, use the session for usability testing alone.

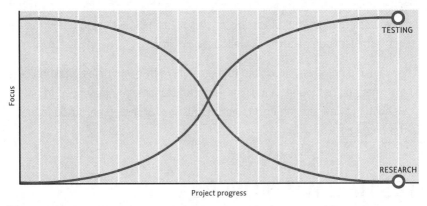

▲ *Use a dual-purpose user session to conduct extra research, phasing in usability testing as you generate designs.*

WHAT TO TEST

What you test will depend on when you test. You might want to begin a redesign project with a summative test of the existing site, and as you start to develop the design, run formative tests with your prototype.

Once you've selected the designs you want to test, write a test script containing the tasks you'll ask users to perform. Your tasks should be representative of real user activity and phrased in an unbiased way. In particular, watch your verbs. A biased task like "Search for the cheapest flight to Europe" will send users straight to the search box, while in real life they may prefer to browse through the site's navigation. If possible, read your tasks aloud to a friend to check that they make sense to a typical user.

As a rule of thumb, allow three times as long for the test as it takes you to run through the tasks yourself. This allows for administration time and the slower pace of your participants. Aim for between 15 minutes and an hour in total. Shorter tests aren't worth the hassle, but longer tests become tiring. If in doubt, choose several short tests over a few long tests.

RECRUITMENT

You can find usability test candidates in exactly the same way you found research participants. Existing customers make for excellent participants, and their opinions are usually of great interest to the business. If you spoke with customers in the research phase, see whether they are willing to return to test the system. Most will appreciate the opportunity, and can tell you whether the new site meets the needs they discussed during research. However, avoid asking research participants to take part in more than one usability test. Their familiarity with the prototype will skew your results and outweigh the convenience.

It can sometimes be tricky to schedule sessions with customers without asking for permission, so don't worry if you have to look elsewhere. Anyone broadly representative of the site's user base can offer valuable insight from the perspective of a first-time visitor. As with your undercover research, don't be shy to grab a friend or a member of the general public if you have to—just consider first whether you need a non-disclosure agreement.

> **NOTE**
> A non-disclosure agreement, or NDA, is a legal document used to ensure that the participant doesn't reveal sensitive details about your prototype. Larger companies can be especially protective of their intellectual property, so you may have to ensure your participant signs an NDA. If in doubt, check with your legal team. They may already have a suitable form—if not, you'll have to seek legal clearance by explaining the business case behind testing and iteration. If the business withholds permission, you have no choice but to skip formative usability testing. Unfortunately it's difficult to introduce UX design to businesses with extremely restrictive legal attitudes.

Again, you should give an incentive to participants. Cash works well, but you might be able to offer something more useful to real customers. For example, if you're testing the purchase process on an e-commerce site, try watching your participants buying a gift of their choice (within a price limit) on a company credit card.

HOW MANY TESTS?

Undercover usability tests are about getting quick feedback on the biggest problems on the site, not generating scientifically rigorous results. Even a single user test is better than none, but the more tests you run, the more likely you'll catch the main issues and eliminate freak results. For a single round of testing, five users will uncover most of the major issues. If you have access to more participants, schedule a second round of testing on an updated version of your site. Budget and time constraints will eventually dictate your testing limits.

VENUE

Although a spare meeting room at the office is an easy venue for usability testing, unfamiliar corporate surroundings can be intimidating for participants. The undercover alternative is to arm yourself with a laptop and head to a local coffee shop. Scout around for a place nearby, not too quiet, not too busy, where participants will be comfortable. If your tasks involve personal information or sensitive behavior (disclosing medical history, for instance), avoid public venues altogether.

Ensure you can access your prototype from your chosen venue. You can bring it with you on paper or the laptop, or you can upload it to a password-protected server, in which case your venue needs reliable Internet access.

TAKING NOTES

Moderating usability tests demands concentration, so it's difficult to take good notes in a test. If you record a video of the test, you needn't worry about missing important details. Ideally you want to capture screen activity along with video and audio of the test participant.

To record tests conducted on a screen-based prototype, there are several software options. Mac users should check out Clearleft's Silverback **B**, an inexpensive guerrilla usability testing tool ($70, www.silverbackapp.com). PC users can turn to TechSmith's Camtasia Studio ($299, www.techsmith.com/camtasia.asp) to record screen activity and video from either a built-in camera or a cheap webcam. Other options include Snapz Pro (for Mac, $69; www.ambrosiasw.com/utilities/snapzprox) and Screencast-o-matic (web-based, free; www.screencast-o-matic.com). The gold standard for usability testing is Morae (for PC, $1495; www.techsmith.com/morae.asp), but at the price it's an unlikely undercover tool.

B *A usability test recorded by Silverback—a Mac-based application we developed at Clearleft.*

If your organization won't let you run unfamiliar software, you can record the session with a camcorder and tripod. Failing that, you'll have to resort to handwritten notes or an audio recording.

If you're conducting a test on a paper prototype, you'll be scrabbling around for the right piece of paper and have even less time for note taking. Ask a colleague to operate the prototype while you direct the test and the participant.

GUEST OBSERVERS

Inviting observers to usability tests can help you show the importance of UX, but if you're an inexperienced moderator you should gain confidence alone first. If you do invite guests, insist that they only ask questions at the end, in a neutral, non-leading way. Unless you have dedicated observation facilities—such as a one-way mirror, or software that can stream the test to another computer—never invite more than two observers. Any more and you risk creating an intimidating test environment where the participant may be uncomfortable about speaking his mind. If you're unable to accommodate observers at a session, send them the recordings and invite them to a future session instead.

ON THE DAY

Print off the relevant paperwork beforehand, such as a list of attendees (including a phone number if possible), a receipt for the incentive, and a non-disclosure agreement if required. You should also provide a consent form—a template explaining the participant's role in the test. Download a sample consent form at www.undercoverux.com/resources.

Arrive early to set up and run a quick trial, leaving enough time to fix any problems. Once your participant arrives, greet her and offer a drink before you explain the purpose of the session and what will happen. Pay the incentive before the test starts, so the participant doesn't feel she has to earn it by pleasing you, and ask for permission to record the test.

> **TIP**
>
> If you're feeling sneaky, here's a little tip to help smooth the path of feedback. Before the test begins, tell the participant that you weren't involved in designing the site, so you won't be offended by criticism. It's a little ethically dubious, but it can improve the candor and quality of the feedback you receive.

Once you're all set, start your recording, give the user her first task, and observe quietly. Encourage your participant to think aloud, explaining what she's doing and what's going through her head. If your participant is struggling, try not to intervene immediately; instead, ask for her opinions so that you can understand the cause of her confusion. If she's still nowhere near the right path, make a note and then step in and help.

You'll find some participants are more useful than others, uncovering dozens of issues, while others will breeze through the test. Some you'll barely be able to get a word out of; others will talk endlessly. Use open-ended "why," "what," and "how" questions like "What do you think this page is telling you?" to encourage quieter participants to talk, and avoid subjective leading questions such as "Do you like this page?" or "Does this button need to be bigger?"

At the end of the test, ask the participant for her general opinions in a quick debrief. Did she enjoy the experience? Was the site easy to use? Did she struggle at any point? Keep an eye open for any trends, and if you're after some quantitative data, ask the participant to rate her experience on a post-test numerical questionnaire.

UNDERCOVER USABILITY TESTING DO'S AND DON'TS

Assuming all goes well, an undercover test is no more challenging to run than a standard usability test. However, the cut-price nature of this testing means there are a few extra concerns to look out for.

Do's

■ Charge your laptop battery. Running out halfway through is a disaster, since you'll probably lose your recording too. Bring a charger if you have access to a power socket.

■ Conduct a thorough trial run. It's embarrassing to find out too late you can't access your prototype outside your company's firewall.

■ Turn off alerts and clear your browser cache and history between tests, particularly if you're using your own laptop. You don't want a participant to read your incoming email, and visited link colors and search auto-suggestions from a previous participant can ruin a test.

■ Have a backup plan. If your prototype doesn't work, turn the session into a research interview. If you're holding a dual-purpose session as outlined above, you can move smoothly into the other phase of the session.

■ Keep a sense of humor. Things will go wrong. Maybe the coffee shop will be unbearably noisy, or the Wi-Fi will go down. Take any setbacks in your stride. You're after quick input, not perfection.

Don'ts

■ Don't follow your test script too tightly or too loosely. You might need to watch the clock, so allow some flexibility without discarding your prepared tasks altogether.

■ Don't over-test. Moderating usability tests is surprisingly hard work. Running more than five tests in one day is pushing it; try to spread your tests over a couple of afternoons or perhaps over a few lunch breaks.

■ Don't be afraid of rejection. Participants regularly don't turn up, and if you're approaching strangers they may prefer to be left alone. Rejection is a peril of the undercover moderator. If you find yourself with a gap between sessions, review the recording of your previous test.

AFTER THE TEST

Immediately after the test, note any important issues while they're still fresh in your mind, but don't worry about creating a comprehensive list. To analyze the tests in detail, set aside some time to run through your recordings, looking for moments when the user struggled to use the site effectively.

Listen carefully to what your participants said as well as what they did. Many usability experts advise against this since people's words can be surprisingly dissimilar to their actions, but if you ignore the subjective comments, you can often glean useful insight into your participants' mental models of how the site works. An inaccurate model can indicate that your design doesn't communicate the site's structure and function well, although users need only understand these well enough to get the job done.

During your run-through, make a note of whether the participants were able to complete each task, the number of errors they made (perhaps splitting these into minor and major errors), and how long each task took. You can easily compile this information into a short quantitative report (see "Presenting Findings," later in this section).

Finally, spend a few minutes evaluating your technique. Did you interrupt the participant? Did you ask leading questions? Should you have allocated more time for a particular task? Make a mental note for next time. As your moderation skills improve, so will the results you get from usability testing.

OTHER UNDERCOVER TESTS

A usability test is a simple way to test your design with users, and it's easily adapted to undercover work. However, you can combine it with other testing methods to get a range of user feedback.

Rapid Iterative Testing and Evaluation (RITE)

Normally you will wait until you've conducted a full round of usability tests before amending your prototype. However, if you're very short on time and need to be more responsive, try RITE, an accelerated usability test method. RITE encourages you to amend the prototype between tests, as soon as you notice a usability issue. This way you can immediately test your improvement with your next participant.

RITE is an advanced technique. Although it allows you to test multiple solutions and improve your prototype quickly, it demands strong technical knowledge, a keen eye for spotting issues during a test, and an appreciation of how to resolve these issues fast. RITE also lacks the balance and rigor that multiple participants offer, making the method susceptible to freak results. However, once you're comfortable with standard testing and confident about pushing your boundaries, RITE is an outstanding way to get more value from undercover usability tests. If you're testing an HTML prototype and aren't confident in your ability to make rapid changes, partner with a friendly developer who can update the prototype between sessions.

Tree test

A tree test ◧ examines the structure of your site and how easy it is to find information within it. Like its cousin, card sorting, it's a straightforward yet surprisingly powerful method. Simply write ten or so representative user tasks on index cards. Then write your primary navigation items on separate cards, and the corresponding secondary navigation on the reverse.

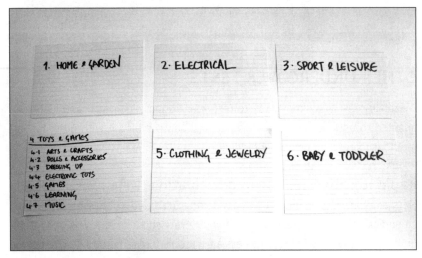

C Use a tree test for a quick assessment of your site's navigation.

To conduct the test, lay your primary navigation cards in a row and ask your participant where he would go to perform the given tasks. When he chooses a primary navigation card, turn it over to reveal the secondary navigation and let him choose again.

Tree tests are an excellent way to learn if items are well placed in the site's structure and if users follow your intended route to particular resources. The method is extremely quick and also lends itself well to remote tests (see section below). It can even help you demonstrate why one site structure is better than another: simply test both versions and compare the proportion of users who find the given information on the first attempt.

REMOTE TESTING

The straightforward setup of face-to-face testing is ideal if you haven't had much experience, but the recent growth in remote online testing offers UX designers new ways to test a site without the need to drag users into the room. Some purists say remote testing loses the nuances of face-to-face interaction, but it offers several advantages for undercover work. Remote tests are fast and inexpensive, allowing you to gather large amounts of user data with little effort. For international or hard-to-reach users, remote testing may be your only viable option.

Remote testing tools range from the trivial to the sophisticated, with price ranges to match. Fortunately most remote tools offer a free trial period, allowing you to try before you buy. Remote tests fall into two main groups: **synchronous** and **automated**.

Synchronous remote tests

Just like face-to-face tests, synchronous tests involve live moderation. You give the participants access to your prototype on their computer and use screen-sharing software to watch them interact with the site. You can talk to participants either through the screen-sharing software or by telephone. The test is run in the same way as a face-to-face test: participants step through a number of predefined tasks, while you note how they use the site and ask for their thoughts as they go.

SCREEN-SHARING SOFTWARE

Screen-sharing software allows you to run synchronous remote tests by displaying in real time what's happening on the participant's computer. Commonly used software includes:

- *Skype (www.skype.com)*

- *Adobe ConnectNow (www.adobe.com/acom/connectnow)*

- *GoToMeeting (www.gotomeeting.com)*

- *LiveLook (www.livelook.com)*

- *Cisco WebEx (www.webex.com)*

Most screen-sharing software will ask the participant to install a small program or browser plug-in. Although the software will guide the process, this can make synchronous testing an intimidating option for participants. Allow extra time for synchronous remote tests in case of technical problems, and avoid synchronous testing altogether if your participants are novice web users.

You need to recruit participants for synchronous tests yourself. Fortunately, you can cast your net wider since geography isn't an issue. For a truly responsive test, try live recruitment using a service such as Ethnio (www.ethnio.com). These services place a short recruitment screener on your site as a pop-up , allowing real users to sign up to participate in a test. (Yes, pop-ups are generally bad for usability, but only a few users will see them, and the end justifies the means.)

D An on-site recruitment pop-up.

When new participants complete your screener, you can contact them to conduct immediate tests. Use the screen-sharing software of your choice and simply watch as they use the site for themselves—it's far more realistic than a scripted set of tasks, and since the sessions are already happening online, it's usually easy to invite observers to watch. If the participant isn't available immediately, you can schedule a session for a later date.

If live recruitment sounds like too much effort, use another recruitment technique from Chapter 2, such as agencies, customer lists, and public forums. Don't forget that you still need to provide incentives for your test participants: electronic gift certificates are easy to distribute over email.

Automated remote tests

Automated (or unmoderated) remote tests don't need direct moderation: you simply set them up and let them run in the background.

AUTOMATED TESTING

Automated testing services are exploding in popularity, and even now there are too many to list in full. Some popular services are listed below—explore them for yourself and see which best suits your needs.

- *Chalkmark (www.optimalworkshop.com/chalkmark.htm)*

- *CommandShift3 (www.commandshift3.com)*

- *Feedback Army (www.feedbackarmy.com)*

- *FiveSecondTest (www.fivesecondtest.com)*

- *IntuitionHQ (www.intuitionhq.com)*

- *Loop11 (www.loop11.com)*

- *Navflow (www.navflow.com)*

- *OpenHallway (www.openhallway.com)*

- *Treejack (www.optimalworkshop.com/treejack.htm)*

- *TryMyUI (www.trymyui.com)*

- *Usabilla (www.usabilla.com)*

- *Userlytics (www.userlytics.com)*

- *UserTesting (www.usertesting.com)*

- *UserZoom (www.userzoom.com)*

- *Webnographer (www.webnographer.com)*

- *WhatUsersDo (www.whatusersdo.com)*

Automated testing tools vary. While many adopt the familiar model of asking participants to step through representative tasks, more experimental tools look specifically at navigation, users' reaction to aesthetics and brand, findability of information, and so on. Some provide videos, some provide written reports of user feedback, and others provide heat maps of user activity.

Many automated services will handle recruitment for you, although this could mean that participants are not sufficiently similar to your intended user base.

MIXED TESTING

Given the benefits and deficiencies of each testing method, it's a good idea to run several different types of test. Perhaps you can combine some corridor testing with some remote automated testing, or conduct some guerrilla usability testing to add context to site analytics (see "After Launch," later in this chapter). Whatever tools you use, testing will not only help you improve the site but also develop your UX design skills. By seeing how users react to designs, you learn to anticipate problems in advance. Testing makes for a better site both now and in the future.

PRESENTING FINDINGS

Unless your tests were completely undercover, you should let your stakeholders know how the sessions went. An email or short presentation is better than a hefty usability report. Open with headline quantitative data: task completion rates, number of errors, scores from automated tests, and so on. This data gives a snapshot of the state of the current design and can help make a tangible business case for testing. Explain, for instance, that a test uncovered usability issues that prevented 40 percent of participants from completing their purchase, and stakeholders will be keen to run further tests. Don't exaggerate the importance of this data, however, as undercover usability testing isn't exactly a rigorous exercise.

Briefly discuss both the major issues and areas of the site that were successful. Use short video highlights to demonstrate these moments—a frustrated or delighted user is more persuasive than any words. Finally, wrap up with a sentence or two on how you plan to improve the design.

★ CRITIQUE

Every UX design project needs the blessing of stakeholders, so once you're confident that your designs meet both business and user goals, it's time to gather feedback from your team.

Everyone has an opinion on design. However experienced a designer you are, your work will be praised by some, and slandered and overruled by others. Criticism can drain a budding designer's motivation quicker than anything else. UX designers therefore need thick skins, without falling prey to the stubborn prima-donna stereotype.

Taking control of the feedback process is one of your hardest challenges, but get it right and you can turn negative, arbitrary criticism into valuable critique. Critique is a structured process in which stakeholders give design feedback based on evidence, logic, and the problem at hand. Critique is a sadly overlooked area of UX design, yet it's critical to the success of your mission to introduce UX. Leading a critique session takes bravery and practice. Inevitably, it also means that you now have to take off the undercover mantle, but don't worry. All the work you've done to this point will help you make the case for good UX design.

PLANNING A DESIGN REVIEW

The simplest way to gather critique is to hold a design review: a face-to-face meeting with key stakeholders. It's easier to explain your decisions in person than in writing, and you'll receive a quick response from attendees, keeping momentum high. However, if your project is less critical or time pressured, as your early undercover projects may be, you may prefer to ask for feedback by email. Some stakeholders won't reply—be sure to find out whether that reflects approval or lack of time to respond.

Design reviews can be intimidating, so conduct a test run first with teammates and any colleagues sympathetic to the UX cause. They'll be able to point out areas that warrant a closer look, and give you the valuable experience of handling feedback.

Attendees

You already identified your important stakeholders during research, so your attendee list should be easy to compile. Generally, the higher risk the project, the more people you should involve. Eight attendees is a sensible maximum for a design review; if you need to consult more, hold separate sessions. At the least, invite your boss and the likely developer to a design review, along with any visual designers or content colleagues who will be working with the design.

Timing

Design reviews fit well into the natural breaks of your project, such as after a round of usability tests or at the end of an Agile iteration, but you will know best when your designs are ready for critique. You may wish to hold a session early in the project to discuss user flows, sitemaps, and page description diagrams, followed by a closer look at the specifics of a prototype.

Keep your session under an hour so attention doesn't wander, but be prepared to allow a couple of extra days for stakeholders to compose any follow-up thoughts. If you're an innie, you may be able to set deadlines for this feedback, since people understand the dangers that bottlenecks pose. Note that this trick doesn't work if you're an outtie: imposing deadlines on a paying client tends not to go down well.

Preparation

It's best to demonstrate wireframes or prototypes on screen, since your colleagues will see the design in its natural habitat. Try to book a meeting room with a projector for design reviews. You can present other deliverables such as sitemaps and storyboards on paper; print out a copy for each attendee.

Plan how you'll guide attendees through the designs, and ensure you can explain the rationale behind every design choice. Many good ideas fail because they're not adequately explained: if your design seems arbitrary, it'll be easy to overrule. Your rationale should of course be based on the context of the project such as your users, the technology, the task you're designing for. Many decisions will also be driven by broader concepts of good design. See "Winning a Debate," later in this chapter, for advice on using this knowledge to reinforce your points.

We recommend showing only one version of your designs per design review. Demonstrating several options can turn design reviews into beauty contests, where stakeholders focus more on picking out their favorite elements than raising legitimate design concerns.

THE SESSION

At the start of the session itself, thank everyone for attending and explain how the session will work. A design review isn't about coming up with answers. Instead, you should encourage feedback (both positive and negative) that addresses the needs of both the business and the user. If you created personas and design principles, introduce them here so that all attendees have a shared understanding of the user and how the design tries to address user needs.

Although you're no doubt eager to open up your prototype and let people at it, to encourage the right kind of feedback you should first explain the context of the design. Summarize your work to this point. What problem are you trying to solve? Who are the users? Have they tested the prototype?

Now, finally, you can show your solution, discuss its various elements, and explain the rationale behind the design. After you've covered a sensible amount, perhaps breaking up complex designs into smaller chunks, open the floor for feedback on what you've covered. The comments should flow freely. Most people find it easier to critique a specific design than discuss abstract requirements, but if folks are quiet, draw out opinions by asking open questions such as "What do you think needs further work?" or "Is this design as effective as it should be?"

You'll typically receive two types of feedback. The first is the type you want: an objective critique related to the project, such as "Is that appropriate for our personas?" or "Our brand guidelines prohibit that." The second, undesirable type of feedback is personal or speculative: "I don't like the colors" or "My mother wouldn't understand that." As leader of the design review, encourage valuable critique and gently discourage subjective opinion by reiterating that you're most interested in feedback based on rationale, the design's objectives, and the users.

If you find that stakeholders insist on dwelling at the subjective level, ask for detail to expose the underlying rationale. For instance, if a colleague says, "I don't like that photo," ask what specifically he dislikes. There's usually a valid piece of critique lingering below this hunch. Perhaps the photo is out of place. Perhaps it doesn't offer the zoom functionality he expected but forgot to mention previously. The clearer your initial instructions and encouragement of valid critique, the more focused and useful your design reviews will be.

That said, some people are simply better at giving critique than others. Lower-fidelity deliverables require a mild suspension of disbelief, and some people will struggle to fill the gaps. There is also a surprising language barrier; it's not easy to express a cogent opinion on a design without knowing design terminology. This means critique will often emerge in the form of phrases that sound irritatingly vague to a designer. With experience, you'll learn what these phrases mean in design terms; here are a few translation tips to start you off.

TRANSLATING STAKEHOLDER CRITIQUE

"It feels busy/cluttered/intimidating" or "I don't know where to click"

This is usually the result of poor visual hierarchy: the important parts of the page aren't being given sufficient prominence. It's a common problem but simple to fix. Try increasing whitespace, reorganizing the page so that the most critical elements are given some breathing room, or removing features or content (ask your stakeholders' opinions on which are the most expendable areas). A page description diagram can help you refocus on the relative priority of the page contents.

"It feels basic/childlike/too sparse"

This feedback represents the opposite attitude: your stakeholder sees too much focus on the primary task and wants more to be made of the secondary details. Try to clarify the importance of various page elements, decrease whitespace, or consider a column-based layout so that other content is brought up the page. However, watch that you retain readability and scannability, and wherever possible test the design with users to give you more information. What seems sparse to a stakeholder can often feel open and unfussy to a novice user.

"There's too much scrolling" or "All this stuff is below the fold"

Similar to "It feels basic," this comment means your stakeholder wants to increase the density of information or feels secondary information is being overlooked. The fold—the imaginary line below which content is off the user's screen—is a hotly debated web design topic. Studies show that users are comfortable scrolling through a long web page, but there is also evidence that users see and remember less information farther down the page. If your stakeholder simply believes that people don't like to scroll online, assuage this fear by explaining that scrolling is a universally understood behavior, and verify the design with usability tests. If the problem is that expected information isn't visible, as above, try to bring this information up the page by using columns, reducing whitespace, or agreeing what information above should be pushed down to make space.

"It doesn't feel like 'us' yet"

This comment could mean that the stakeholder is struggling to imagine how a low-fidelity deliverable will end up, and needs more visual or textual detail. If this isn't the case, it means the design's visual aesthetic or written tone of voice is inconsistent with the stakeholder's unspoken sense of the brand.

To pin down what a stakeholder believes the brand to represent, create a short list of scales **E** labeled with two opposite extremes and ask where the brand should sit on each scale. Use the results to create a higher-fidelity deliverable, working if possible in conjunction with visual designers and content specialists.

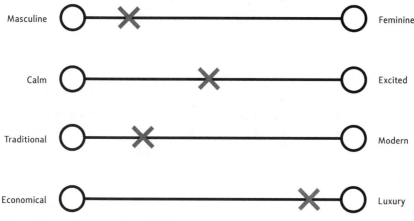

E *Use sliding scales to reveal a stakeholder's perceptions of the brand.*

"That's not how eBay/Facebook/Google does it!"

This retort means your stakeholder doesn't yet trust your design skill and would rather rely on design patterns established by the big boys. They may, of course, be right—so look closely at how the problem is tackled elsewhere and whether it would work in your scenario. It's likely that users will be familiar with the system and thus it could improve your usability. However, if you believe the external solution won't work, explain that the site in question has different user and business goals than your own, so simply copying their solution wouldn't be appropriate.

Here's a secret: big companies employ mediocre designers as well as excellent ones. There's no guarantee that a solution is right just because it's on a famous website. It might just be there because no one got around to changing it.

"Make it sexier/more whizzy/more innovative" or "It doesn't have the wow factor yet"

Comments like these usually reveal that your stakeholder hasn't yet adopted the user mindset and is still projecting her own preconceptions of what the site should be like. Ask her to explain specifically what she means by the term she used, and if she can give an example of a site that does it well. You can also ask (amicably) exactly what user and business objective the change will help to meet. Sometimes you'll find the objection evaporates; if not, continue to drill down on the specifics and consider how you can include them in subsequent designs, or even just in the way you explain your design rationale in the future.

"It needs to pop!"

This is usually a figure/ground problem, meaning the focal elements again struggle to be seen against the less important ones. Recap what exactly should be the focus of the page and bring this element to the fore by positioning it more centrally, using highlight and shadow, or improving contrast through color. A visual designer can be a great help when resolving this issue.

"I know what I'll like when I see it."

This dangerous phrase effectively translates as "Read my mind!" At worst, it can trigger a wild goose chase of variation after variation that ends only when one party gives up in exasperation. Explain that this route will waste time (and cost a great deal of money), and therefore, it's essential to agree on a clear direction.

This response could also suggest that your stakeholder expects the site to be perfect before launch. We've already given several reasons why this is impossible: take your pick and try to convince your stakeholder to let go of the notion.

COMMON CRITIQUE PROBLEMS

Design reviews get easier with practice, but a number of pitfalls await the unwary designer.

What, not how

Focusing on solutions rather than problems is a common mistake. Steer your colleagues toward what should be improved (for example, "The call to action should be more visible") rather than how it should be improved ("Make the button bigger"). Explain that every issue can be resolved in several ways, and it's best to take the time to explore which option works best. For now, avoid committing to any specific user-interface amendment and instead pledge to find the best way of responding to your stakeholders' feedback. The phrase "OK, I'll look at that" promises you'll take charge of improvement but keeps you agnostic about the specific solution.

Taking it personally

Avoid becoming possessive of your designs and you'll become a far more effective user experience designer. Taking criticism personally forces you into a defensive and obstructive role that can seriously harm your cause. Critique is an important part of a designer's life—and there's no better way to learn than by immersing yourself in it.

Feedback at the wrong level

Try not to drift toward minutiae. The level of detail you're after will be guided by the fidelity of your deliverables and stage of the project, but don't assume that stakeholders will immediately understand your work. Be prepared to answer basic questions about your deliverables (such as "Why is this wireframe gray?") and explain what still needs to be completed before the design can be considered final.

If you find your design review spiraling into detail you're not yet concerned with—for instance, typography and images—refocus the group through reference to your objectives, requirements, and unrequirements. If, however, the conversation expands into broad questions like "Why should we have a website in the first place?" you shouldn't ignore these concerns. Pause to ensure the group agrees on the answer before proceeding. (You do know the answer, right? Hopefully you found it in your stakeholder interviews.)

Endless feedback loops

Perpetual cycles of "One more thing" can drag a design into the ground. If this becomes an issue, try rephrasing the focus of your design reviews. Instead of "What do you think?" ask "What needs to change to get your approval?" Once you have the answer, make the necessary changes and consider the design signed off. If that's a little too brave for you, run your changes past the team one last time, but explain that since you've accommodated their requests you're now ready to move to the next phase.

Some unfortunate souls feel the need to suggest improvements to any design, no matter how good, to demonstrate their power. A dirty trick to limit the damage these people cause is to deliberately add an obvious mistake to your work. It's the old "honeypot" scam—by luring them toward the obvious improvement, you hope they'll leave everything else alone. It's devious, and we don't exactly approve, but desperate measures are sometimes necessary.

WINNING A DEBATE

Although critique should be constructive and impartial, it's inevitable that at times you'll disagree with the feedback you receive. Critique is a crunch moment for the undercover designer—you're sticking your neck out and taking the lead of the design process. However, stakeholders sometimes see design as a complex, unpredictable subject that can cause havoc in the wrong hands. Who wants to let a bull loose in their china shop?

To bring UX to the heart of the business, you must persuade colleagues to trust your opinion and expertise. We'll discuss ways to increase your UX responsibilities in the next chapter, but be aware for now that handling critique well is an important way to earn trust. It's easy to undo your hard work with rash disagreement. Never dismiss stakeholder feedback out of hand. Every designer makes mistakes, and there will always be approaches to a problem that you've not considered. The worst UX designers are those who succumb to the arrogant conceit that stakeholders are design-illiterate fools. It's true that your business colleagues may not be able to express ideas in the same visual way you do, but smart stakeholders are always an advantage for a UX designer.

If you're skeptical about your stakeholders' requests, try them out anyway, then do it your way too. It takes longer, but you'll gain trust by showing you can listen to feedback. You may be able to persuade your stakeholder why your design is stronger, or you may even find that his suggestion was better all along.

Nevertheless, sometimes you'll disagree with stakeholder feedback so strongly that you have to take a stand. To defend your case to a stakeholder, we recommend a systematic method of proof we call the Validation Stack **F**.

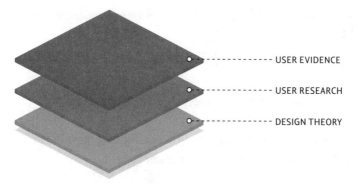

USER EVIDENCE

USER RESEARCH

DESIGN THEORY

F *Use the Validation Stack to defend a design.*

The Validation Stack shows tiers of evidence in order of their relative power. The top tier shows your most powerful ally: data gleaned directly from users, such as usability testing or usage metrics. When you want to win a debate, see if user evidence supports your argument. Did the design test well? Do the figures show that people are using the site in the way you'd expect? If you ran usability tests before the design review, this extra information will give a good design a stronger chance to survive critique.

If you don't yet have direct user evidence, refer back to your research and any design principles that resulted. If you shared this work with stakeholders earlier, they should already have agreed to support its recommendations. If you kept this work undercover, now's the time to pull out the details to support your case.

If your recommendation isn't supported by user evidence or research, you can still support your case with theoretical principles. Businesspeople are often surprised to learn of the scientific foundations that underpin good design. Perhaps your design demonstrates clear information hierarchy, follows the recommendations of Fitts' Law, or uses the psychology of social proof to encourage user behavior; learn about these and other principles, and you'll have a final trump card to play. However, remember that theory is the bottom tier in the Validation Stack. Always choose a theoretically inferior design that tests well over a "properly designed" alternative, and only lean on theory for support when you have no other data.

Finally, if your recommendation isn't supported by user evidence, research, or theoretical principles, throw it away. You've lost this one.

'PROVE IT!'

The Validation Stack is often enough to convince a reluctant stakeholder, but one counterargument is especially hard to defeat: "Prove it!" Colleagues often wheel out this defense to counter your objection to something detrimental to user experience: an unnecessary field in a signup form, or more advertising on a cluttered page. "Prove it!" challenges you to demonstrate that the harm to UX will outweigh the business benefit of adding these elements.

Although the cumulative damage of a hundred bad decisions is obvious, quantifying the effect of a single user-hostile change is much trickier. One approach is to view the challenge as a welcome opportunity to conduct further user testing, or to put both versions live and compare the metrics (see "After Launch," later in this chapter). However, you can also make a theoretical case for why even a single bad UX decision harms the business, using a concept we call the FY Threshold.

The FY Threshold is an entirely unscientific model of how much hassle users will take before giving up on the site (an event often accompanied by a profane remark). Let's say your site currently annoys 10 percent of your users so much that they give up—in other words, it pushes 10 percent of your users beyond their FY Thresholds. Your job as a UX designer is of course to reduce this percentage by eliminating frustrations.

However, decisions that harm the site experience will counteract your work, pushing more users beyond their FY Thresholds. People who would otherwise tolerate the site's issues will give up in frustration, costing you revenue. One apparently minor change can be the last straw for some users.

FOLLOWING UP ON CRITIQUE

After your design review, gather the feedback and circulate it to the team, explaining with rationale which feedback you'll act upon and which you won't. This extra work reduces the chance you'll forget something, shows courtesy to your stakeholders, and provides a record of feedback and your eventual decisions. Projects with several critique rounds have a worrying tendency to produce contradictory feedback after sufficient time; recording it will save you hours if this happens.

If critique has gone well, it shouldn't be too painful to revisit the design in light of stakeholder feedback; only when you feel you've lost out does rework become a chore. Try out some new ideas and work the successful ones into your deliverables. You may need to gather more test data and stakeholder feedback on these new designs. Only you will know how many rounds of iteration you'll need—but try to iterate quickly so you don't lose momentum.

★ AFTER LAUNCH

You've worked hard to refine the site, test it with users, and get stakeholder approval, but UX design is only abstract speculation until you launch. Once the site goes live, you'll quickly learn what works, what doesn't, and how you can continue to make things better.

As we declared in the manifesto, the undercover UX designer cares about delivery, not deliverables, so you still have plenty of work to do once your designs have been signed off. You'll need to work with visual designers, content specialists, developers, and project managers to ensure your work becomes a reality. We'll look at how to support your colleagues as they assemble the site in Chapter 6.

The decision about when and how to launch probably won't be yours. Instead, it will be the result of a delicate mix of business factors such as deadlines, technical risk, and support resources. Some software experts, particularly those who advocate the Agile mindset, recommend launching early and often, and tweaking the site in response to user feedback. However, we UX designers tend to want more certainty before pushing the site to users. Given our passion for putting people first, we're embarrassed to impose immature work on users.

The best answer lies between the two extremes. Launch too early and you'll be unable to do justice to your research and ideas, but launch too late and they'll have passed their sell-by date. The secret is to launch expecting to change. Fire-and-forget sites, pushed live, never to be touched again, tend to be the worst UX offenders; it's your job to prevent this fate befalling your site. Cost is of course the main barrier to post-launch changes, but a site that becomes slowly irrelevant as user needs evolve can cause even greater lost revenue. Convince your stakeholders that owning a website is like owning a house; with attention, repairs, and perhaps the odd extension, it can accommodate their changing needs for years.

To fuel this discussion, you have two new sources of information once you launch: user feedback and metrics.

USER FEEDBACK

It's logical that user experience designers should embrace user feedback, but it can be surprisingly difficult to turn customer reactions into useful design suggestions.

Your first step is obviously to make it easy for people to give their thoughts. You could use a simple feedback form, a blog post with comment fields, or a dedicated customer-service application like Get Satisfaction (www.getsatisfaction.com)—although you'll need to moderate any public channels. Ask your customer service reps to note down any customer comments or bug reports, and monitor any official complaints. Finally, set up a Google Alert (www.google.com/alerts) for mentions of your organization, and keep an eye on social networks like Twitter (www.twitter.com) to see how users are responding. If there isn't a great deal of feedback forthcoming, don't be shy to ask for it. Offer an incentive if you like, but be aware you may attract bogus feedback from people only interested in winning the prize.

Since you're not in direct contact with customers, you won't be able to steer them toward impartial critique, so you'll end up with a lot of diverse personal reactions. The nature of this feedback will depend partially on your site's size and your organization's relationship with customers. Users of a small, unknown site are usually receptive to change that helps the site grow in scope and popularity. However, longtime users of established sites often resist change vigorously; look at the vocal public reaction to redesigns on any major news or social networking site for examples. Where resistance occurs, the course of negative feedback often mirrors the Kübler-Ross model of coping with grief:

- Denial: "Why did you change it? It was fine the way it was."

- Anger: "My 12-year-old could have done better! I'll never use this site again."

- Bargaining: "At least give us the option to use the old version."

- Depression: "I used to love this site . . . "

- Acceptance: "Actually, I've been using the new design for two weeks now and . . . "

We don't mean to belittle the legitimate concerns of users, but it's surprising how often these stages appear in user feedback. To an extent, users are indeed mourning the loss of the previous site. Their mental models have expired, and users may be worried that the site will head in a direction they don't approve of. Keep an eye out for this pattern of feedback; there may even be occasions when you can predict it in advance and forewarn your stakeholders.

Wherever user feedback comes from, handle it with grace. Acknowledge and thank even your most vocal detractors for their feedback. You may wish to point them gently toward your customer service team or assure them that their feedback will be taken into account for future versions, but don't make promises you can't keep. You should base your decisions on repeated patterns in feedback, rather than a single complaint (however vocal).

OPEN DESIGN

Although you'll typically gather feedback once the site is live, in some situations it can be worthwhile seeking user feedback on designs in progress. You could invite a group of core users to give their feedback on upcoming designs, or even retain a dedicated user group to give continuous input. You can even take user involvement to the extreme of **open design***, in which the user community critiques every decision, and the designers visibly act upon on this feedback. Open design is an advanced method that involves extensive diplomacy and community management. It's certainly not undercover. Consider the extent to which you want to gather user feedback for your project, but be aware that handling unstructured user feedback can be time-consuming and politically fraught.*

METRICS

Users will only give feedback if they're motivated to speak up—whether in praise or scorn—but metrics reflect users' unspoken opinions. Earlier, we touched on examining site analytics to get a snapshot of how people are using your old site; after launch, visit your analytics software again, to get an idea of how people are using your new design. Compare this data with your earlier baseline, and you'll better understand whether you've met your intended objectives.

Numerical and analytical aptitude might not come easily to the typical UX designer, but in the target-driven business world these skills are a strong advantage. Metrics give you a starting point for determining the return on investment of UX design, which we'll discuss in the next chapter as a powerful way to get the business hooked on design. Learning some basic statistics would be an excellent time investment, but if you're not mathematically inclined, see whether other people within the businesses can help with analysis. An alliance of strong analytical skills and excellent design skills can be unstoppable.

However, data isn't a panacea. Metrics are like a crying baby: they leave you in no doubt that something is wrong, but don't tell you how to find and solve the problem. To understand what's causing the issue, always supplement numerical analysis with qualitative information from usability testing and user feedback. Design, after all, is not a science. Although you can measure fundamental usability concepts such as process completion and error rates, user experience is also concerned with emotion, enjoyment, and desirability. Trying to quantify these abstract concepts is like weighing love. Let numbers inform your design process, but remember that intuition and empathy should also play important parts. Data can be a powerful means of showing the value of UX to your business, but it can also be used to strangle creativity.

Which metrics you analyze will depend on the goals you identified and the objectives you set. Use the site analytics list given in Chapter 2 to start you off, and add any that you've identified as key measures of the project's success. Before gathering this data, however, allow sufficient time for the smoke to clear after a large redesign. Redesigns almost always cause metrics to slump temporarily since user behavior takes a while to stabilize. By all means, peek at your analytics immediately after launch, but allow at least a week before you take the data seriously. If page views and time on the site dip for a few days, wait to see whether it's a long-term trend.

MAKING CHANGES

It's tempting to push out a quick change to address user feedback and alleviate issues suggested by your metrics. If the newly redesigned sections are cash cows, it's likely you'll also be under pressure from your stakeholders. Don't panic. Negative feedback may be a natural temporary reaction to change, the analytics data may not have recovered from the slump, and there may be a hundred happy users for every vocal complainant. Even if the problems are legitimate, handle user feedback and post-launch usage data like any other critique data. The remedy may be surprisingly simple. Take time to find the right solution, rather than rushing into a knee-jerk fix that could make everything worse.

Bowing to every change request is a surefire way to end up with an unfocused, unusable site, so consider each request carefully against the Validation Stack. Do you have evidence that negates the request? Users can be surprisingly understanding of courteous, rational rejection. If you decide not to pursue a user's suggestion, be polite but state your reasons honestly. Perhaps you believe their idea would dilute the focus of the site, or negatively affect other users. If the feedback reveals a valid concern, revisit the design process to consider an intelligent fix. A small tweak to the interface or its copy may do the job, or you may have to step back to try some new ideas or conduct more research.

As a last resort, when a new design fails conspicuously, you may have to roll back your new design to a previous version. It's a sure way to placate the most critical users, but it usually runs contrary to the interests of site growth and business goals. How harmful rolling back will be depends on your company's attitude to failure. We all know the rhetoric that innovative businesses must celebrate failure, but let's get real. Most companies hate failure. Scrapping your designs can be highly embarrassing, and for the undercover designer it's unlikely to be a positive step toward UX adoption.

Some successful web businesses never revert new designs, relying instead on a belief that users will calm down and use the new design happily once they see its benefits. It's a risky and somewhat arrogant strategy, but if you're certain of your research and testing, and are prepared to put your neck on the line, it might just work.

A/B AND MULTIVARIATE TESTING

To optimize the site or test the waters before committing to a new design, many businesses turn to A/B and multivariate tests. These tests let you compare multiple versions of the same site by randomly displaying different versions to users and analyzing the aggregated results. If you're testing variations of a single page element, it's called an **A/B test**. If you're changing multiple elements of the page, it's a **multivariate test**.

Some businesses conduct A/B and multivariate tests manually by creating two versions of a page and balancing traffic so that approximately half the users see one design and half the other. This doesn't scale well to tests with many variations, which would require Herculean design and development efforts. Instead of doing things the hard way, try out tools such as Google Website Optimizer (www.google.com/websiteoptimizer) and Performable (www.performable.com). Give these tools the designs or parameters you want to test and the metrics you want to monitor, and the software handles the tricky traffic balancing and provides a summary of performance data.

Like remote testing, A/B and multivariate testing can be compelling allies for the undercover user experience designer, taking some of the pain out of holding large-scale tests yourself. They excel when used to optimize an already good design, particularly on areas of your site that depend on quantifiable user actions, such as downloading software, signing up, or completing a purchase. Calls to action and "microcopy"—snippets of instructional or persuasive text—are particularly well suited to A/B and multivariate tests; different wordings will resonate surprisingly differently with users. You can also use these tests to gauge the effect of simple interface tweaks such as the position, wording, and appearance of a call-to-action button, or the layout of two sections of marketing copy.

For all their strengths, A/B and multivariate tests are also prone to misuse and are therefore controversial within the UX field. Since these tests are statistical procedures that examine the behavior of a sample of users, there is always a risk of misreading the results. In particular, A/B and multivariate tests should be **statistically significant**: that is, conducted with a large enough sample that the chance of a freak result is minimized.

These tests are also prone to the common failing of quantitative feedback: they will tell you which designs perform better, but not why. A/B and multivariate tests do very little to build design expertise; if you rely on them as the only source of validation, design is reduced to a series of wild stabs in the dark in the hope that the numbers go up. That's not UX design; it's guesswork.

Finally, while A/B and multivariate tests are great at optimizing an existing design, they won't help you radically improve your site. Instead, they will help you refine the design until it reaches what's known as a local maximum **G**.

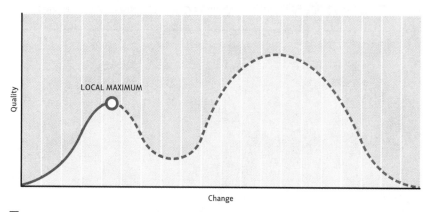

G A/B and multivariate testing can help you reach a local maximum, but won't help you design a radically improved site.

The **local maximum** represents the optimal state the site can reach without radical redesign. A/B and multivariate tests will suggest small changes that bring you closer to this maximum, but if you're always looking for fractional improvement, you'll miss the opportunities that bold reinvention can offer. To reach new heights, you need to have faith and accept that new designs may perform worse than the local maximum until you iterate enough to realize their full potential. As the proverb suggests, you can't jump a 20-foot chasm in two 10-foot leaps.

Given these pitfalls, run A/B and multivariate tests with caution. As long as you back these quantitative findings with qualitative user testing methods, you'll be able to smooth off the rough edges of your website with relative ease.

REFINING YOUR SOLUTION: FURTHER READING

- *Remote Research: Real Users, Real Time, Real Research*, by Nate Bolt and Tony Tulathimutte (Rosenfeld Media, 2010)

- *Rocket Surgery Made Easy: the Do-It-Yourself Guide to Finding and Fixing Usability Problems*, by Steve Krug (New Riders, 2009)

- *Handbook of Usability Testing: How to Plan, Design, and Conduct Effective Tests (2nd edition)*, by Jeffrey Rubin and Dana Chisnell (Wiley, 2008)

6

WORKING WITH...

So far, we've described a rather idealized user experience design process, but you'll find that real projects don't run so smoothly. The design phases, neatly divided here into chapters, are fluid. You'll find yourself flipping between phases, returning to supplement earlier work, and roaming through the project in your own way. This is natural. Although every designer follows his own skeletal design process, successful designers tweak their processes depending on context: the medium, the budget, the constraints, and their own personal style.

We've also presented the process in relative isolation. Colleagues, culture, and politics naturally make things messier. The human angle is critical to undercover UX design, and working well with others will prove as important as applying your design skills.

The easiest way to get along with others is of course to get to know them. There's no substitute for spending time with people. Understand your colleagues' personalities and outlooks and you can anticipate how they will respond to your work. You might even make some friends along the way.

However, getting to know people this well takes years, and you can't wait that long to get started on your undercover UX mission. Fortunately, while individuals vary, certain groups within a business tend to share similar traits and attitudes. We caution against making sweeping assumptions about your colleagues, but considering their likely motivations, possible causes of conflict, and ways to arouse their interest in design will help you drive UX adoption.

★ WORKING WITH DEVELOPERS

The fields of design and development are yin and yang, complementary yet opposed. They rely on each other, and thus either support or damage the quality of each other's work. Poor execution in development can ruin the experience you've worked so hard on.

Your relationship with developers is one of the most important you'll form, but too often the relationship is characterized by tension and distrust. Fortunately, it needn't be this way.

THE DEVELOPER MINDSET

Good developers are hardwired for efficiency. In their working practices, as with their code, they minimize effort wherever possible. Don't mistake this for laziness. Developers work in a medium that rewards efficiency, and they look for the same rigor in the world around them. However, some developers may not appreciate that others don't think the same way. Empathy is not always a developer's strongest suit. Some developers will create an elegant code model, and then claim that this is all you need for a usable site. Designers know that revealing the innards of a system is rarely a sound choice, but it can be difficult to convince resolute developers. Even if you are able to communicate the UX benefit, developers may still resist compromising the code structure for what they see as minor improvements, giving the defense "it doesn't work that way."

Developers take pride in creating code that performs, scales, and most important, works. But strong developers also have a pragmatic desire to make the business's ambitions happen online. Herein lies the perennial tug-of-war of web development: quality versus business pressure. Development teams are the punching bag of the business, forced to make last-minute changes by oversights or poor business decisions. To stay sane, developers have built up defense mechanisms and resist anything that prevents them working at their best. Faced with lack of involvement, project bottlenecks, or ambiguity, developers can take a defensive and even obstructive stance when estimating workloads and feasibility.

Most developers also harbor a keen dislike for arbitrary decisions. They will typically demand rationale before accepting a decision. You should therefore invite developers to design reviews and offer to answer their questions as they build the site. Many developers view building a site as a matter of finding creative technical solutions to business problems, and they'll gladly contribute their thoughts on how the site's design shortcomings can be addressed.

GETTING ALONG WITH DEVELOPERS

You will find it easier to convince developers of the value of UX if you view them as partners, not adversaries. Adept developers already appreciate the importance of user experience, and they'll make excellent partners for your undercover UX efforts.

That said, be aware that developers don't *need* UX designers. When the pressure to deliver is on, developers will route around any perceived bottlenecks, yourself included. The remedy is to make yourself indispensable to the development team, and make their lives easy in whatever ways you can.

First, involve developers early in the design process. Include technical representatives in your stakeholder research, and invite them to collaborative design sessions, usability test reviews, and so on. Not all will attend, but those who do could very well become more receptive to your ideas and spread the UX message throughout their team. Solicit developers' opinions on feasibility early, and listen carefully to their responses. Finding out too late that your beloved design is technically unrealistic is hugely frustrating. Since developers are well versed in the capabilities of the system, they can quickly kill off nonviable ideas, and may suggest a better alternative.

Be ready to compromise on some details and fight for others. Given developers' time constraints, they often question whether visual nuances like rounded corners are necessary. If you believe these elements will have a strong impact on UX, explain your case, but be aware that by sacrificing purely aesthetic choices, you may free time to focus on more important UX specifics.

Sit near developers if you can, so you can be in regular contact about deliverables, ambiguities, and progress. As you sketch out ideas, ask developers for their feedback, and discuss the format and fidelity of your final deliverables. Be sure to communicate design decisions, and subsequent changes to them, through design reviews or annotations to your deliverables. Without this communication, developers may be tempted to ignore your designs, thinking them arbitrary. In return, ask that they show you development work in progress so you can comment on any subtleties missing from the execution. Since developers often work at high speed, you might need to prompt them to share what they've built so far.

Developers spend much of their time coding defensively, ensuring the site can cope with unusual scenarios and a wide variety of user inputs. Therefore, pay attention to special cases such as error states and the behavior of the site for visitors without JavaScript. If site content is generated from user actions or input, what happens before this content exists? Have you fully described how results pages should work when there are no results to display? Have you explained how to paginate long lists? Have you defined hover states, and do your deliverables explain how to handle text treatment like bulleted lists? Inexperienced designers frequently overlook these details, leaving the developer to either make an educated guess or refer back to the designer.

Finally, to truly understand the world of the developer, step into their shoes. Decent HTML and CSS knowledge will open up powerful prototyping options and help you appreciate the possibilities and restrictions of modern web development. It will also give you insight into the complexity of your designs, but be careful not to second-guess developers' estimates, and don't make the mistake of asking developers to make a change "because it should only take 30 minutes." Just like UX designers, developers operate within tight constraints, such as supporting older browsers, using existing code libraries, and accommodating specific technologies. Although HTML and CSS skills will help you discuss development tasks in the right way, the developer is the boss when it comes to estimation.

> **NOTE**
>
> If you believe developers are producing inflated estimates, try to establish whether caution or deliberate obstruction is the cause. Ask the team to explain where the complexity lies, so that you can make a better judgment next time. You should find it relatively easy to spot the difference between a valid, reasoned argument and blustering obfuscation. If you are convinced that developers are being deliberately obstructive, raise the issue with your line manager.

Taking the time to learn development basics will improve your effectiveness as a UX designer. You will learn to consider the feasibility of your designs, make swift decisions on trivial or impossible ideas, and design in modular fashion so developers can reuse code where possible. Learning the basics also has the pleasant upside of improving your standing in developers' minds, turning you from a potential nuisance into a genuine ally.

OUTSOURCED DEVELOPERS

In recent years, many organizations have chosen to outsource web development to inexpensive overseas companies. Like many such cost-cutting exercises, outsourcing creates extra indirect costs. Without direct access to the developer team you will struggle to evangelize the role of UX in good development practice.

Coding standards will instead be driven explicitly by the agreed contract and the documentation you provide.

Where development is seen as an entirely downstream function, the only way UX ideas can make headway is if they are baked into deliverables. Work at extreme detail and fidelity, so that the outsourced team has no alternative but to follow your instructions. Companies that outsource development make for a challenging UX environment. These organizations usually regard quality as a lower priority than cost, meaning the potential quality gains from great UX design may not be persuasive.

MOVING FROM DEVELOPMENT TO UX

If you're currently a developer, you're well placed to make hands-on improvements to the site. If you think you can improve on the design you are asked to build, ask your stakeholders how it was reached. The decisions with which you disagree may have been oversights or deliberate choices. If there is scope to try something different, try building it the way you believe it should work—without spending too much extra time—and demonstrate the amended version. Explain why you believe your version is more effective, and the likely business benefits of the change. Lightning-quick corridor usability testing will strengthen your case. Your colleague may tell you to stick to the specification they gave you, but they may also welcome your help and agree to your recommendation. Keep this momentum up, and stakeholders will soon adopt the habit of seeking your advice on UX design issues.

★ WORKING WITH VISUAL DESIGNERS

UX design can be conceptual. Spend weeks in the abstract realm of user needs, structure, and navigation, and it's easy to forget that the job's not done until the design is made visible. Enter visual designers, who give voice to our thoughts by producing detailed designs and graphics for the site.

A good user experience involves many elements that fall into the realm of visual design, such as aesthetic appeal, emotional response, and creating a strong first impression. Visual designers offer more than mere decoration; they can make your design speak with a visual language of its own.

THE VISUAL DESIGNER MINDSET

Visual and UX designers lie at opposite ends of the same spectrum. Both are natural problem solvers, but while UX designers focus on the foundations of the design, visual designers concentrate on the visible surface. This role involves juggling many different elements, such as color, visual hierarchy, texture, shape, typography, and composition.

Designers with backgrounds outside the digital realm can bring fresh angles to their work, but unless they learn the medium, they may fail to grasp issues such as accessibility, onscreen legibility, and browser support. Most visual designers also favor a certain style of design and a particular fidelity. Some are most comfortable working with broad brushstrokes, creating vivid concepts and pushing in many visual directions. Others are uncomfortable with this level of ambiguity and are happier paying fine attention to the details of alignment, typography, and the grid.

GETTING ALONG WITH VISUAL DESIGNERS

The litmus test of visual designers—as with UX designers—is whether they can articulate the ideas behind their design with conviction and rationale. Good designers accept feedback positively and invite others into the creative process. Bad designers view design as an act of solo artistry.

If you're lucky enough to work with a top-notch visual designer, the partnership can be formidable. You'll learn a great deal about design and your partner can improve the quality of your work through informal critique. However, if you work with a weak visual designer, you'll find life more difficult. Work closely to improve the quality of your joint output, but if your ideas are being regularly ignored or squandered, you may have to adopt a more combative stance. Working at a very high fidelity gives a weak visual designer less freedom to make mistakes.

You should of course take the time to learn the language and theory of visual design. It will help you communicate with visual designers and make you a better UX designer, but remember that theory alone doesn't make you a visual design specialist. Respect the boundaries between the UX and visual roles, and draw the line at the appropriate place for your skills and mutual comfort zones. Visual designers who work best at a conceptual level won't appreciate being locked down by high-fidelity wireframes. Those who prefer to focus on detail will be uncomfortable working from a rough sketch. Generally, less experienced designers should create clear boundaries of responsibility, while experienced practitioners can step into each other's worlds more comfortably. If boundaries do become a problem, causing UX and visual designers to tread on each other's toes, adopt different approaches to fidelity and deliverables. A page description diagram (see Chapter 4) or a rough prototype may be more acceptable than a detailed wireframe, leaving the details of layout in the hands of the visual designer.

UX and visual designers should jointly own the design process, running design reviews together and regularly asking each other's opinion on work in progress. When giving feedback on visual designs, adopt the same attitude you request from stakeholders, relying on reason rather than subjectivity. Ask your visual designer why she made the decision in question; the answer may be unexpected and enlightening.

Given every designer's instinct to push boundaries, visual designers may occasionally underestimate constraints and suggest unrealistic solutions. Your stakeholder and user research will help you bring these ideas down to earth and steer the design down a more plausible path. You may also need to remind visual designers to concentrate not just on the "perfect" state of a page, but also on special cases such as text wrapping on long headlines, empty page states, and how the design scales at different sizes.

MOVING FROM VISUAL DESIGN TO UX

Given the proximity of the UX and visual design fields, it is relatively easy for a visual designer to adopt UX techniques. The combined UX-visual role is broad, stretching all the way from research to the final design. You should therefore be adept with all aspects of UX and visual design, and learn to prioritize your work to avoid becoming overwhelmed. You'll also need to know the visual design software of your choice inside and out to create both designs and UX deliverables quickly.

★ WORKING WITH CONTENT SPECIALISTS

Until recently, content has been the poor relation of other digital disciplines, downtrodden, forgotten, and under-resourced. Considering content provision someone else's problem harmed the user experience cause, while bottlenecks, rushed content, and failed projects saw mediocrity triumph.

Fortunately, the pendulum is at last swinging back to its rightful place, where content is seen as a central part of the planning and design process. It shouldn't have taken so long. Users come, stay, and return for content; and however fantastic your design, bad content will ruin the user experience. It's therefore in your interest to help your content partners produce their best work.

THE CONTENT SPECIALIST MINDSET

Everyone thinks they can write. The web content specialist therefore faces difficulties you're already familiar with, such as explaining the benefits of high-quality professional material over amateur work. The content-creation process and the design process are similar in many ways. Both UX designers and writers respond to an incomplete brief, shape ideas into an initial direction, and refine those ideas based on critique. Your content colleagues will have experienced many of the same pressures as you, and you'll be able to swap countless war stories of unrealistic deadlines and unhelpful feedback.

Having been victims of bad process for too long, content professionals want the business to adopt new methods that allow sufficient time to audit, plan, write, and edit content in time for launch. Like developers, they dislike redundancy in both their words and their working habits; poorly planned work means more content to create, more pages to manage, and a confused message.

GETTING ALONG WITH CONTENT SPECIALISTS

Your first priority when dealing with content staff should be to improve processes together. Content strategists make natural leaders of this exercise, asking difficult questions about process and strategy. What should the site say? To whom? How often? They will also want clarification on how the organization judges content success. Does the business want to generate traffic? Or inbound links? Or customer engagement, measured through comments, sign-ups, or repeat visits?

Pay close attention to the answers, since these strategic goals may be indistinguishable from UX goals. Try to ensure that your undercover UX work points in the same direction.

A writer can cover a topic in a hundred ways, so offer whatever user insight you have available to help them choose the best approach. Qualitative research outputs such as personas, along with any advice you can offer about users' language and mental models, will help writers plan and produce effective text that appeals to and persuades the site's users.

Content professionals can provide invaluable input throughout the design process. In the early stages, they can explain content requirements such as the nature of content you must accommodate (text, video, or images), its source (internal, third-party, or user-generated), and any points of written style to which you must adhere. Content specialists make natural partners for your initial content audits, and can act as judges of content quality. As you sketch out ideas, they can clarify the intended message and the calls to action of a page. The content team will also know what metadata surrounds their content—for instance, author, topic, date, and audience—potentially giving you new navigation approaches such as "More articles on this topic" or "Today's most popular downloads." Finally, ask writers what lead times they need to produce content of sufficient quality, and make sure they are brought in at the appropriate time. This may be before development starts.

Organizations that invest in content professionals usually provide them with a content management system (CMS). A CMS will introduce notable technical and process constraints to a project. Ask to be trained on the CMS to understand its capabilities, and learn how its workflows are reflected in the business itself. Attempts to bend these constraints, such as a large-scale content restructure, are typically doomed by hefty administration or customization costs, even if the software itself is open source.

Not all organizations have the luxury of a dedicated content team. Content is often written by marketing or communications teams, who are juggling dozens of responsibilities and aren't web writers by trade. These people may not be able to lead the content cause in the way a professional content strategist might, but they'll be glad of any improvements you can initiate.

★ WORKING WITH PRODUCT OWNERS

Products—and their intangible cousin, services—are the things businesses offer their customers. If you're working on a web application, this might be the business's primary product. For example, the value of social networking sites, online email clients, and photo-sharing applications comes from the site itself and its features. Most of the time, however, the website isn't the product itself; it's a way to see, review, and buy products, which could be physical (books, for example) or intangible (loans).

Wherever the product lies within the business, it needs someone in the driving seat to make day-to-day decisions. In a small organization or startup, this may be the role of the managing director, but in larger companies this responsibility is delegated to a domain specialist. If you're working in-house, this role is known as the "product owner." If you're an external consultant, you probably just call this person your "client."

Large companies have many product owners, each responsible for a group of products that meet specific needs of specific customers. These groups are often known as "verticals." For example, a publishing company may produce books for schools, universities, and industries. These verticals are likely to have different needs and different products, and hence have different product owners.

Even if product owners are not directly responsible for the website, they wield strong influence since the website is an important means of accessing the product and explaining its value.

THE PRODUCT OWNER MINDSET

Product owners tend to be domain experts. They know the industry, its history, its market forces, and its trends, and use this knowledge to shape the development of the product and their entire organization.

Pressure is a fact of life for product owners, and their heads are often the first to roll in the event of failure. Product owners invest their emotions in their work, and may lose sleep thinking about ways to succeed in a competitive market. This emotional involvement is a double-edged sword. Product owners are deeply committed to the well-being of their product, but they can take criticism personally.

Product owners must articulate clearly what the product does, what need it fills, and why it is the right choice for customers. They should also have a vision of the future of the product. To conceive this vision, a product owner combines market and sales information with experience, ideas, and hunches. The vision may range from compelling and viable to wildly unrealistic, and from widely known to held solely in the product owner's head.

Product owners typically embrace new ideas if they offer a way to differentiate the product. However, success can transform some product owners into risk-averse absolutists, driven by the fear of failure or losing face.

GETTING ALONG WITH PRODUCT OWNERS

A weak product owner poses a formidable obstacle, but a smart product owner can bring your UX dreams to life. Get cozy with product owners and you'll learn the inside track on the business case, competitive landscape, and market trends behind the products that make your business. You'll also learn their personal motivations. Whether they're chasing a promotion, a surefire success, or an inno-vative long shot, part of your role is to make product owners happy, particularly if they're external clients.

It's important to agree on a shared vision for the site as well as the product. Your product owner is probably the stakeholder with the most to say about the future, so pick their brains extensively in your research. As you move through the design process, air your own thoughts about the site vision, and try to reach a shared understanding of how the product and the site should look in a few years.

Product owners are often responsible for measurement; how else will they know if their vision has been achieved? Try to agree on objectives and metrics that represent both business success and UX success, so that you can weave good UX into the future of the product.

Your relationship with the product owner will influence your approach to fidelity and critique. Product owners are usually impatient to increase fidelity, since detail better communicates how closely the design will match their vision. Feel free to share low-fidelity deliverables that reflect the essence of the site, but be prepared to push product owners for their thoughts on these incomplete concepts.

As custodians of product features, product owners may also assume responsibility for website features. Ideally, their requirements will be based on a rational understanding of the business and customer environment, but they may be equally driven by a knee-jerk reaction to competitor activity. UX designers and product owners clash when one disagrees with the other's analysis of the situation. Designers accuse product owners of being seduced by glossy features that are worthless to users, or of blindly copying competitors without considering the suitability of their approaches. Product owners accuse designers of refusing to accept business reality and putting their aesthetic preferences above the good of the product. Both arguments contain a kernel of truth. Stand up for your opinions, but try to minimize conflict by empathizing with a product owner's viewpoint.

Although product owners may not officially outrank you, don't underestimate the strength of their positions. They can and will overrule you, and will usually receive management support to do so. Product owners make a bad choice of enemy. Feel free to air your opinions, but be ready to cede minor UX points to stay on your product owner's good side. Thankfully, good UX work usually appeals strongly to product owners. They dream of a desirable product that people love, buy, and tell others about, just as you do. Given the common ground, you should have little difficulty wooing your product owner. Once your relationship grows, you can amicably lock horns on important issues, and you might occasionally get your way.

Product owners naturally want to get involved in everything, so they can appreciate progress toward their goal. This energy keeps them driven, but it can also turn them into meddlers. Keep product owners away from the kitchen, and explain that they should focus on the "what" and leave the "how" to you. Don't let them dictate your methods, and encourage them to give their feedback through official critique.

Research is a common cause of friction. Product owners may confuse design research with market knowledge, and their broad understanding of the market—what people are buying, the features that are most in demand, the actions of competitors—may lead them to conclude that more customer research is pointless. To make the case for design research, explain that their aggregate industry knowledge is useful when creating business and marketing strategy, but less valuable for design. Instead, you want to learn about individual behaviors and how the site and product will fit into someone's life.

★ WORKING WITH MARKETERS

UX design and marketing make obvious bedfellows, since traditionally most businesses regard marketing teams as the guardians of both customer knowledge and web strategy. The relationship is accentuated by the similarities between UX and the concept of *brand*. A misunderstood term, an organization's brand is far more than just its name, logo, or promotional aesthetic. A brand consists of the associations, both rational and emotional, that ordinary people make with the company. While marketing teams can help to create these associations through advertising and careful consideration of how the company presents itself, brand is deeply affected by a customer's personal encounters with the company—in other words, their user experience.

Brand equals user experience plus non-user experience; that is, it consists of your customers' opinions and your potential customers' opinions. These experiences are shaped by every contact someone has with the business: customer service, commercials, packaging, shipping, and yes, the website. In time you may choose to bring your UX focus to all these customer touchpoints, but for now, know that successful undercover UX work on the site will help to build a better brand.

THE MARKETER MINDSET

Marketers thrive on research and data that add to their customer knowledge. They use this information to identify trends and capitalize on them, creating marketing messages and approaches that people will respond to. So that the scale of this data doesn't become overwhelming, marketers combine their information-hoarding tendencies with a precise focus. They believe, as do UX designers, that targeting specific user groups is a more productive strategy than trying to serve everyone equally.

Marketers are aware of the persuasive power of content and design, and see the web as an excellent channel for connecting with customers. However, marketers spread their eggs across several baskets. This provides insurance if any channel proves ineffective and allows marketers to try new approaches with little risk.

Since customer awareness of a product and its benefits takes a while to grow, marketing is a game of persistence. Its practitioners need to keep banging the drum, but the results do come, with sufficient time and money.

GETTING ALONG WITH MARKETERS

We've already discussed in Chapter 2 how to use market research within UX design. Marketing data can form the skeletons of data-driven personas, inform research recruitment strategies, and enlighten you about the demographic and psychographic makeup of your users. However, you should be aware of the limitations of marketing data, and it's likely you'll want to conduct your own research. Be careful when explaining this request. Never get into a fight with a marketer about who knows customers better; you'll lose even if you're right. Instead, position your requests for more research as a way to supplement marketing knowledge with personal stories and the human touch that helps you design for the individual user.

Marketing team members will want the site to demonstrate the company's **brand values**, a set of simple principles and attitudes that encapsulate the organization's personality. If these values have been embraced by the business, this is an easy task: features, content, and design will naturally reflect the internal culture. More commonly, however, brand values haven't permeated the organization fully. In these cases, brand values are harder to express. Interview marketing stakeholders to learn how they wish to present the business, and explore the tone used in offline marketing material.

While brand values can help you create design principles and guide your design and content, a company's brand values are often sadly indistinguishable from those of its competitors. E-commerce sites, for instance, all want to be known as quick, simple, trusted, and comprehensive. Without brave or even polarizing brand values, it can be hard to create a truly differentiated design. It's easier to stand out by defying convention rather than following it, and a compellingly different set of brand values will help you design a more memorable site.

Businesses often run web redesign projects in parallel with rebranding exercises. On the surface, this can seem like a smart move: both sides can influence the other, and the refreshed website can lend extra impact to the new brand launch. However, concurrent redesign and rebrand projects can create their own difficulties. At worst, these dual projects grind to a halt, with neither team committing to their designs for fear of the changes the other will introduce. These stalemates usually reflect a lack of understanding of the teams' roles and disciplines. In these situations, pause and revisit the groundwork. Both web design and brand teams should explain their processes, work conducted to date, and any areas of overlap that are worrying them. Try to end the discussion with clarity on the next steps and mutually agreed decisions on boundaries in responsibility. Ideally, each party should stick to their strengths. Few brand experts are also web experts, and web designers tend not to appreciate the many nuances of branding.

UX designers and marketing teams should anticipate disagreement on two specific sections of a website. The first is the homepage. Every design project must balance user needs and brand needs. A site that is too brand-driven will feel more like an advertisement than a useful site, but a site without any brand presence will struggle to explain why it matters. This push and pull is most keenly felt on the homepage. Expect your marketing colleagues to press to have key messages appear prominently, and expect that you will resist this attitude as overly pushy. Compromise and user testing are the only two reliable resolutions to this tension.

The second potential flashpoint between UX designers and marketers is user input. To marketers, sign-up forms are golden opportunities to gather extra data, allowing the business to segment and target users better. To UX designers, any unnecessary question increases the likelihood of user frustration and abandonment. Listen to marketers' requests and then examine every potential question in detail to find out who will use the resultant data, and for what purpose. If the question is being asked more out of curiosity than for a compelling business reason, make a strong case for its removal. If there are still sticking points, you may have to A/B test a couple of versions of the form to compare the relative sign-up success rates.

Despite these minor differences of opinion, marketers generally hold UX design in high regard. Should you need to convince them further, look for ways to frame UX goals in terms of marketing targets. A good user experience will directly affect customer acquisition, retention, word-of-mouth referral, and loyalty.

★ WORKING WITH SEO SPECIALISTS

At first glance, there appears to be little common ground between the disciplines of search engine optimization (SEO) and UX design. SEO is concerned with getting users to the site by ensuring the site can be found using the right keywords on the right search engines. UX mostly focuses on what happens on the site itself. Perhaps SEO specialists own the user before they reach the site, and pass stewardship to UX once they arrive?

There's also an apparent philosophical conflict, with SEO professionals and UX designers pulling in opposite directions. SEO specialists want to optimize the site for machines—that is, search engine spiders—while UX designers want to improve the human experience with the site.

Fortunately, the views can be reconciled. Experience is blind to boundaries. It doesn't begin when a user lands on your site, nor does it end when they leave. UX designers should take an interest in how someone finds their sites, and pay close attention to the seams between offsite and onsite experience. And while a few of the less principled SEO techniques can directly conflict with UX goals, reports of a fundamental schism between the two practices are greatly exaggerated.

Search companies want the same thing as UX designers—a web full of great sites that meet users' needs—and search engine algorithms can be seen as an attempt to quantify the user experience of the site. What is the site about? Is it easy to navigate? Which pages are the most valuable? Who thinks this site is good enough to link to? Tellingly, Google's self-professed number one principle is "focus on the user and all else will follow" (www.google.com/corporate/tenthings.html).

THE SEO MINDSET

The SEO industry attracts opinion like no other, and is lauded and vilified in equal measure. In recent years, charlatans have leapt onto SEO's success and undermined the discipline through low-quality work and underhanded "black-hat" SEO techniques (see sidebar).

However, don't be put off by the few bad apples. Avoid blanket prejudice and assume your SEO partners are the good guys. Quality SEO work shows excellent return on investment and gains serious traction in business.

Like UX designers, serious SEO specialists want good websites with findable, valuable content. It's easier for an excellent site to place highly in search engine results than a mediocre one. All an SEO professional asks is that sites be designed and built with consideration for the needs of search engines. A search engine spider is in essence your lowest-tech user. It does not understand JavaScript, cannot interpret images, and blindly follows links until it gives up and goes elsewhere.

If this user can't use the site, your site will have search engine problems. SEO specialists therefore prefer well-defined site architectures, good metadata, and extensive links between content.

BLACK-HAT SEO

Black-hat SEO (as opposed to white-hat SEO) uses unethical techniques to trick search engines into ranking sites more highly. Black-hat techniques include hiding keyword-stuffed text in invisible colors or positioned off-screen, creating doorway pages full of phony text, and cloaking—that is, presenting different versions of the site to search engines and real users. If your SEO colleagues are using black-hat techniques, blow the whistle immediately. Search engines spend millions of dollars on detecting black-hat techniques. Eventually your site's transgressions will be punished with removal from search indexes, with serious financial implications for the business.

SEO professionals fear not having any influence over large architectural issues such as major redesigns, in which one careless mistake can undo many months of effort. In situations like this, the SEO team typically gets the blame anyway and is stuck with the difficult task of picking up the pieces.

GETTING ALONG WITH SEO SPECIALISTS

Involve your SEO colleagues in information architecture work. They will want to see sitemaps and user flows, and will frequently suggest improvements or areas where your proposals could damage the site's SEO potential. It's generally desirable to create a unique page for every category and product (if that makes sense from a UX perspective), but watch out for structures that create large numbers of duplicate pages, which can carry an SEO penalty. Try to link extensively to key pages, perhaps using simple navigation items such as a footer or breadcrumbs, and fix broken links as soon as possible since they harm both UX and SEO.

The humble URL plays a large role in SEO. Start discussions about URLs early, since they'll also affect information architecture and development strategies. Technical platforms and content management systems will have a strong influence on your URL structure: discuss your needs with developers to see what is possible. Generally, search engines prefer fairly flat hierarchies that include key-words in URLs. For example, http://sitename.com/products/x1-allegra-energy-saving-lightbulb is likely to be a better URL for SEO purposes than http://sitename.com/content/catalog/2010/bulbs/energysv/x1. Once you have agreed on a URL convention, include the intended URL as an annotation in your wireframes to ensure consistency. Watch out for dynamic sites, which can make developers' lives easier but cause major difficulty for SEO specialists.

NOTE

Pages created dynamically are built on the fly, while static pages sit on the server waiting to be accessed. Think of it like a restaurant: is the meal cooked to order, or precooked and taken from under the heat lamp? Dynamic sites can cause problems for search engine spiders; consult closely with developers and your SEO team to minimize the risk.

The quality and structure of developers' code will also have an SEO impact. You may prefer to stay out of this conversation altogether, but if you are confident in your skills you may be able to offer insight on the page's HTML markup. Spiders respond effectively to well-structured code, and give extra priority to page ele-ments such as headers. To further help the visiting spiders, include alt attributes on images, and provide descriptive text for links.

Although UX specifics deep within the site are less relevant to SEO specialists, they will be interested in "seam" pages such as landing pages. Knowledgeable SEO input can help you craft better landing pages by explaining the keywords users entered to find the page.

Content decisions also have a natural SEO impact. Wherever you consult with your content colleagues, consider inviting a search specialist along. As well as knowing what a page should say, and to whom, it is helpful to know what search keywords people will use to find it. Writers may be concerned that SEO employ-ees will ask them to stuff their content full of keywords to improve SEO perfor-mance; fortunately this practice is now deprecated and considered borderline black-hat. Well-written content naturally contains the right keywords, although your content team may wish to introduce a couple of alternative phrasings to catch searches for less common terms. Pay particular attention to page titles, which should be straightforward and descriptive.

Your organization's SEO and search engine marketing (SEM) strategies can reveal a great deal about the user experience you should design for. What keywords will the site compete for? Do these represent the "long tail" of less popular search terms, or more expensive and competitive phrases? Are visitors likely to be looking for something specific, or browsing out of uncommitted curiosity? Consider whether your site design will suit the sort of user you expect to arrive from search engines, and whether SEO goals make sense in light of your design research. Consider adding keyword phrases to your personas, and suggesting useful keywords based on your site search analytics.

Due to the mutual benefits between the two disciplines, you may be able to smuggle UX improvements under the guise of SEO (with the search team's permission, of course). However, driving traffic to the site is like pouring more water in the top of your funnel; it may simply amplify any UX problems you have and make your site's leaks more obvious. It might be better to make the case for making UX improvements before turning up the search engine volume.

★ WORKING WITH SENIOR MANAGERS

Managers come in many varieties. Most commonly, you will deal with middle managers overseeing a specialized department, such as marketing or IT. They have disparate skills and outlooks, driven largely by their area of expertise. To understand them, look elsewhere in this chapter; we focus here on senior managers and executives.

Your interactions with managers of this level may be brief, but they count. Senior managers have the power to crush your fledgling UX movement—along with your morale—but they can also promote the cause in a way you only dreamed of. Help a senior manager to fall in love with UX and your quest is almost won.

THE SENIOR MANAGER MINDSET

We all know that executives are busy. They juggle many aspects of the business, of which the website is just one. They must shift their attention between pressing tactical concerns and complex strategic matters, without letting any issue blind them to another. It's a pressured role. Their superiors, the board, and shareholders expect them to make the decisions that assure a company's success.

A senior manager's most precious resource is timely and concise information. They appreciate their employees getting to the point and presenting options backed up with supporting evidence. They dislike people making important decisions without their input, and equally they dislike being pestered over trivial decisions. However frustrating your undercover UX mission, resolve your difficulties without recourse to a senior manager. Airing your grievances will label you a troublemaker and undermine your cause.

GETTING ALONG WITH SENIOR MANAGERS

Make your interactions with managers as painless as possible. Give them the information they need to make a decision, and no more. Executive summaries are so named for a reason; give senior managers extensive reports and they will flick through but not read. Present managers with facts rather than speculation— customer research, analytics, and testing data will prove invaluable when explaining user experience issues.

There's little point approaching a senior manager with only problems. After explaining the current situation, present potential resolutions and explain the benefits and downsides of each. Anticipate your executive's likely questions and prepare concise answers, and your efforts will be appreciated. Become known as a diligent employee who gets to the point and does their homework, and you will be in an excellent political position. Earn a manager's trust and they will consult you more frequently for advice, allowing you to slowly introduce them to UX. Like the rest of us, managers can be inspired by new ideas, so once you have a good relationship with a senior manager, try to pass on a little of your passion. Point out how other companies have solved long-standing problems through design and technology, in the hope that you will spark within your manager a lasting interest in UX design.

A manager's time and information constraints mean there's no need to expose the inner workings of your design process. As the economist Theodore Levitt said, "People don't want to buy a quarter-inch drill, they want a quarter-inch hole." Managers are largely unconcerned with how you achieve results, and an earnest explanation of the theory of UX will fall on deaf ears. Only explain the detailed UX design process to a manager if they ask (a sign that you may have piqued their interest). Senior managers will also show little interest in your deliverables unless they can directly see how they will affect the end product. Where you do need to seek their opinions on your deliverables, present as high a fidelity as you can.

This advice extends beyond deliverables to all your UX dealings with senior managers. While you may be motivated by value-led goals such as making better products that people will love using, senior managers care most about business performance. To make a convincing case, frame your UX discussions in terms of business benefits, such as:

- Reduced risk. UX practices such as research and usability testing can help reduce the risk inherent in all projects. Ask the senior manager, "How important is it that this site works right?" and use the response to make the case for reducing risk by spending a little more time consulting with users.

- Enhanced user knowledge. Executives appreciate the importance of understanding customers, since research reveals opportunities for more effective marketing, better product differentiation, and innovative product development. Senior managers can feel so wrapped up in the goings-on of the business that they feel isolated from genuine customer knowledge. Explain how your UX research techniques will teach the business more about current market and social trends, and help the business achieve better results from its web strategy.

- Better compliance. Regulatory compliance can be a powerful motivator. In some cases, poor user experience can cross the line of legality, invoking the threat of legal action. Accessibility concerns in particular are now heavily regulated, and related legal challenges are forcing even the largest companies to take action. If you notice an area where UX design could alleviate the risk of legal difficulties, make an urgent case and you may find your request is accepted with few questions asked. Not only can you reduce the threat of legal action, but also by designing for universal accessibility you ensure that the company's services are accessible to all, increasing the company's potential market.

- Time and cost savings. This argument may appear counterintuitive to senior managers who see design as a bottleneck that slows down development. However, robust research can reduce the time spent refactoring code later, thoughtful design can reveal straightforward development approaches, and thorough testing can resolve the ambiguity that often dogs the latter stages of a project. Time to market can be the factor that makes or breaks an innovative service. While there's no such thing as a free lunch, you can save money if you eat a hearty breakfast.

You should know how to relate every weapon in your UX armory to a business benefit. If you can't, spend some time working this out, and write down your conclusions. The benefit need not be directly quantifiable; brand perception and customer loyalty, for instance, are frequent outcomes of UX design. This exercise not only arms you with compelling ammunition for requesting UX work, but also attunes you to ways you can highlight the success of your work. Managers value employees who make a difference. Try to start your projects by showing some quick, noticeable results, and only then embark on the details of the full project. Measure the success of your quick wins, and if you save or earn the company money through UX, tell management. If you're shy about your achievements, you're only starving the decision makers of information that can help your cause. There's no harm giving executives something to brag about, and it spreads the word of your UX success.

Senior managers will frequently make decisions that disappoint you. There's a chance you didn't state your case well enough, but it's more likely that they had more information than you, or were subject to conflicting pressures. Don't be disheartened if it takes a while to get senior managers talking about UX, and don't get too carried away if you think you're starting to make progress.

★ WORKING WITH AGILE

Finally, we come to not a role but a way of life. Over the last few years, the Agile mindset has taken hold in many digital businesses, and it is now a factor in many designers' working lives.

Agile was born as a reaction to the heavy-handed and often impractical demands of so-called "waterfall" projects, in which businesses create software in discrete phases: research, design, build, and test **A**.

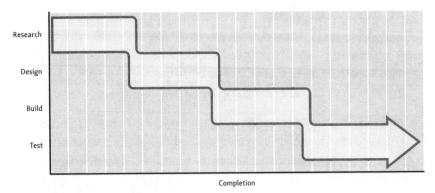

A *Waterfall projects require design work to be completed before the site is built.*

Agile replaces this serial process with a nonlinear method that encourages collaboration between departments and rapid, iterative design and development **B**. Rather than specifying a system's behavior in full before it is built (known in Agile circles as "big design up front"), Agile proponents select certain user journeys and develop the system iteratively, both building new sections and revising previous work.

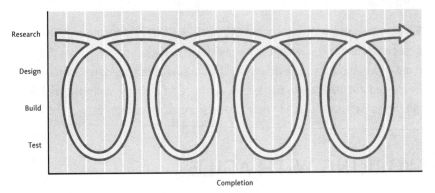

B *Agile projects involve design and development working in parallel.*

The growth of Agile has caused problems for some designers. The method's origins lie in internal developer-led projects that paid little notice to design. However, contemporary Agile practitioners are eager to redress this balance, and introducing high-quality design into an Agile environment has become one of the largest intellectual and practical challenges facing the UX field.

The main cause of friction is that UX design and Agile reflect two different mindsets. UX designers are predictive. We want to make great systems by understanding users and their needs, and designing the right system for them. Agile adherents are reactive. They accept that change is an inevitable part of any project, and choose to develop quickly and accommodate rework where necessary.

Agile projects put extra pressure on design since they demand quick turnarounds; often only a week or two for each iteration. Some designers therefore claim Agile circumvents their processes, leaving no time to conduct research or agree on a coherent vision with stakeholders. Agile environments can also become heavily developer-led, leaving designers disempowered. These accusations are true to an extent. Agile methods make for a substantially different design environment than that of waterfall methods, and Agile designers must find ways to work quickly, take the odd shortcut, and push in UX techniques wherever they can.

Fortunately, that's what this entire book is about. Every undercover UX technique is compatible with Agile methods, and we contend that designers have nothing to fear from the Agile mindset. Undercover UX design requires a quick, results-driven approach that embraces occasional ambiguity in the knowledge that iteration will smooth out the kinks. The only appreciable difference with Agile methods is that Agile brings development into this iterative cycle. Instead of iterating on deliverables, designers iterate on a real site.

Agile brings the many people working on a project into more visible contact. It advocates cross-functional teams in which every employee understands each other's role and solves problems collaboratively. This open communication makes it easy to assert the benefits of UX design, and gives designers unrestricted access to the partners—developers, product owners, visual designers, and more—who can make UX ambitions a reality. The old "us versus them" mentality won't fly in an Agile world.

TIPS FOR AGILE DESIGN

The first thing to realize is that Agile is chiefly a mindset, not a process. The mindset commits to building software early, to testing marginal decisions by putting them live and watching what happens, and to free communication based on conversation instead of documents. The techniques that surround Agile—such as pair programming, daily Scrums, and user stories—are merely artifacts of this mindset. Try to become comfortable with the Agile way of life rather than focusing on specific techniques. Just like our undercover manifesto, Agile prefers a good product today to a great product next year, making perfection even less realistic. Instead, strive to make pragmatic design decisions, and take comfort in the knowledge that you can rework areas that don't perform well.

Although Agile projects don't allow much time for up-front research, you can negotiate a decent preparation window by starting with an "iteration zero." This is a short phase at the start of the project that precedes any development. Developers often use this time to set up development environments and work on back-end functionality like setting up databases. Use this time to conduct some quick interviews or surveys so you can create some simple personas. Present these to your team at the end of the iteration zero, and substitute your personas into your user stories.

> **NOTE**
> A user story is a short description of system functionality, stated in the terms "As a [user role], I can [user task], so that [user benefit]." Your personas make excellent replacements for the user role: "As Jim, I can log in to my account so that I can check my balance and any payments due."

The iteration zero will undoubtedly leave many questions unanswered, but you can conduct more research once the project is underway, using the dual-purpose session discussed in Chapter 5.

The Agile mindset eschews all but essential documentation, preferring direct communication between team members. Choose your deliverables carefully, omitting any that aren't entirely necessary; make low-fidelity your default; and consider your deliverables to be fluid documents. Although you won't be designing the entire system in advance, you'll typically design the coming iteration's work while supporting developers as they build the current iteration. Try not to fall behind and become a bottleneck or, equally important, get too far ahead, since your work might be wasted. The design effort required for each iteration will vary, which can make time management a challenge. Agile iteration plans are usually based on developers' estimates of upcoming work; try to establish a similar estimation process for your UX work. Nevertheless, some iterations will prove particularly frantic.

To ensure a coherent vision throughout the project, you should appraise continuity from time to time. Review the site at regular intervals (try to squeeze in quick user testing, too), and judge whether the site experience is consistent across the site. Agile is iterative, not just incremental, so if you notice UX problems with previous versions, raise them with the team and put the user story back into the backlog so it can be revisited.

Popular though it may be, the Agile mindset provides no guarantees. Successful Agile needs experienced teammates who not only excel in a fast-paced environment but also collaborate effectively with other specialists. Fluidity is essential. In Agile teams more than ever, you cannot act as the sole custodian of UX. Although you should be the final decision-maker on UX design issues, you should involve the whole team in the design process, using the collaborative techniques discussed in Chapter 3. The best Agile teams are multidisciplinary and multiskilled. At these levels you may even spend some of your time coding, writing copy, doing visual design, and so on. The future of Agile will see everyone pitching in and playing well with others.

WORKING WITH: FURTHER READING

- *Building Findable Websites: Web Standards, SEO, and Beyond,* by Aarron Walter (New Riders, 2008)

- *Selling Usability: User Experience Infiltration Tactics,* by John S. Rhodes (Rhodes Media, 2009)

- *Designing with Web Standards,* 3rd Edition, by Jeffrey Zeldman and Ethan Marcotte (New Riders, 2009)

- *Content Strategy for the Web,* by Kristina Halvorson (New Riders, 2009)

- *Zag: The Number One Strategy of High-Performance Brands,* by Marty Neumeier (New Riders, 2006)

- *Getting Real: The Smarter, Faster, Easier Way to Build a Successful Web Application,* by Jason Fried, David Heinemeier Hansson, and Matthew Linderman (37signals, 2009)

- *Google Webmaster Central help pages, www.google.com/support/webmasters*

WHERE NEXT?

We've focused on the practical aspects of the UX design process, but the undercover UX struggle also has to be fought outside of these tactical battlefields. High-quality design deliverables will excite some of your colleagues, but how can you interest the rest of the business and convince your stakeholders to give budget, responsibility, and recognition to the UX cause?

THE UX ADOPTION LADDER

As we warned in the manifesto, large-scale cultural change is slow. Despite the familiar rhetoric of change, companies generally evolve sluggishly, but with time the persistent evangelist can help colleagues see the light of UX. In most organizations the route of progression is remarkably similar.

Phase 0: undercover UX

A business at this stage of user experience adoption hasn't heard of UX, so user-centered design doesn't feature among its priorities. The organization is typically more concerned with managing costs, matching competitors' features, or handling logistical or process issues. The user is regarded as a consumer of the company's products, a sales target, or at worst a nuisance against whom the site should be safeguarded. Feature requests are usually driven by perceived marketing needs. Where UX work does materialize, it's performed by rogue individuals under the guise of the regular web design process.

Phase 1: emergent UX

In this phase, UX ideas are beginning to take root in the organization, and the team is shedding its inward focus. The organization may informally regard a staff member as a usability specialist, and may make a small budget available for usability testing. However, UX is considered a veneer to be applied at the end of the web development process, and the business applies only a few basic tools as part of this pre-launch "check-up."

That said, some stakeholders have begun to take an interest in UX, although their knowledge of UX techniques is unsophisticated. The user is referenced in internal discussions, although the organization's knowledge of the user is perfunctory. Ersatz users are often used to discuss the appeal and usability of new features: "My mom wouldn't understand this."

Phase 2: maturing UX

A business approaching user experience maturity appreciates that UX is more than just validation of the site's usability. Instead, UX has gained a strong foothold in the company's digital output, and an executive-level champion formally recognizes the cause. The organization employs at least one dedicated UX practitioner, who is given an appropriate job description and performance targets. UX training is available to help employees keep their skills fresh, and there may be plans to recruit more internal UX talent, or to commission external consultants for specific projects.

The organization has a reasonable UX budget and can choose from various methods and tools depending on the project at hand. UX specialists are brought onto project teams early enough to conduct light research and generate ideas. Employees may have developed an informal design style guide, and senior UX staff may have formal sign-off responsibility for the site.

Phase 3: integrated UX

The organization has now adopted a user-centered focus that stretches beyond its digital activities. Senior leaders understand the benefits and methods of user experience practice, and have agreed on a UX strategy that complements the wider business strategy. User needs drive new product development, and the company's understanding of customers is current and thorough. Iteration is embraced as part of the design process. User experience is believed to be the responsibility of all employees, although UX specialists are valued as an integral part of the company.

CLIMBING THE LADDER

The methods detailed in previous chapters naturally drive UX adoption. Using the insight and results of the design process, you can change attitudes, educate your colleagues about the importance of the field, and become regarded as an essential part of your company's digital strategy.

However, you can only ever take an organization up the ladder one step at a time. No matter how impassioned your approach, it's impossible to take a company straight from UX indifference to UX maturity. The demands are too disruptive. Focus, as the undercover manifesto suggests, on big change through small victories, slowly winning hearts and minds and convincing your team of the need for UX approaches.

Take ownership

No one will win the UX case for you. Although it can be tempting to succumb to exasperation over your colleagues' lack of interest, taking ownership of the problem is more effective than playing the victim. Make UX your personal mission and persistently champion the cause. Your first step should be to get UX responsibilities added to your job description; you'll probably have to write these additions yourself and persuade your manager to approve them.

Back up your newly-gained responsibility by requesting personal UX targets such as improving the company's Net Promoter Score. While these targets will also be subject to factors outside your control, they can provide powerful evidence for the positive impact of your work.

However, job description and targets alone don't make you a UX designer. Remember the manifesto—we believe in action, not words. Make sure you're actually being given the time to fulfill your new UX responsibilities. You may even have to volunteer for jobs that aren't part of your job description, such as testing or writing copy, to keep the UX momentum high.

Win allies

Work to assemble a gang of UX-friendly allies. Start small, one individual at a time, and as you gather momentum, try to convert whole teams to the cause. A loyal group of partners will smooth the path of UX adoption by evangelizing user needs in your absence, by proposing improvements to the site, and by consulting you on decisions that would otherwise pass you by.

With sustained growth, UX methods will sprout between the paving stones of the business. You're now ready to take the case to senior management. Hold a joint intervention, explaining that you've been using these methods successfully, showing your work and results. Ask the business to give its formal support to UX, be it through budget, sign-off responsibility, or even the appointment of an official UX team. Your aim is to position UX design as a groundswell, less easily ignored than the ranting of a lone troublemaker.

Educate

Share your UX passion and expertise. For example, hold an informal lunchtime meeting to analyze a recent redesign of a competitor site, discussing what is good for users and what is likely to have a negative impact. Or create a monthly UX newsletter in which you discuss external UX trends and highlight your current work. Try streaming your usability tests and inviting your colleagues to watch, or upload videos of test highlights to the intranet.

Alternatively, use your design skills elsewhere in the business. For instance, every company has plenty of poorly designed forms; spend just a couple of hours tidying these up, and you will show firsthand the benefits of design and earn a favor from your colleagues.

These tactics may seem trivial and even desperate, but early in your UX quest they can be effective. If you subsequently find yourself too busy with "real" UX work to keep these efforts going, don't worry. It means you're moving in the right direction.

Persuade

At times you'll be asked to convince stakeholders directly of the benefits of UX. Your ability to persuade others with a convincing argument will be critical to your success. Psychologist and author Robert Cialdini describes six "weapons of influence" that drive persuasion and trust.

- Reciprocity: people like to return favors. Look for ways to make your colleagues' lives easier, and they'll be more inclined to accommodate your future requests.

- Commitment and consistency: people are more likely to complete a goal once they have committed to it. Use this concept to consolidate both design principles and design reviews. Sending follow-up emails summarizing group decisions will encourage people to commit to the decisions and discourage them from changing their minds later.

- Social proof: people are more prone to do things that others are doing. Use this principle to draw attention to the adoption of UX in other businesses through case studies, competitive analysis, and so on. Look carefully at any competitor redesigns and highlight the user experience impact to alert stakeholders to the increasing adoption of UX techniques.

■ Authority: people are more likely to obey people in positions of authority. You may not yet hold this authority yourself, but enthuse a senior stakeholder about UX, and he or she will spur adoption throughout the business. The concept also applies to authority of knowledge: demonstrate a deep understanding of the topic, and your opinion will be more highly regarded.

■ Liking: people are more apt to obey people they like. We've already covered what makes different teams tick, but take some time to learn about your colleagues on a personal level. Beer helps. Knowing your colleagues well will help your cause and, more important, make it more fun to work with them.

■ Scarcity: people are more likely to take action in the face of high demand and scarce supply. Look out for opportunities to promote UX as an in-demand competitive advantage in your sector.

These techniques will prove all the more effective if you have included stakeholders in the design process. This collaborative mindset permeates the whole undercover UX process; if stakeholders have contributed to the solution, they'll be more inclined to see it go live.

Show return on investment

You should find it straightforward to explain why basic UX design matters. Your argument is simply a matter of highlighting fundamental UX problems from your initial exploration—expert reviews, corridor tests, competitive analysis, and so on—and making the case that customers are being driven away by these issues. In these early stages, the strongest case for UX is one of fixing mistakes and plugging the resultant revenue leaks. However, once the most conspicuous issues are resolved, these logical arguments begin to fall short. To approve further user experience work, the business will want to know that UX design will generate additional revenue that exceeds its cost. In other words, the business will want to know UX's return on investment (ROI).

ROI is the holy grail of not just UX design but almost any design field. Unfortunately, a watertight business case would be pure fiction. Design can yield astonishingly profitable results, but how can you accurately predict the financial outcome of such a creative, complex act?

You will nevertheless be expected to try. Your most reliable method uses quantitative data—analytics data, conversion rates from A/B and multivariate tests, survey data, and so on—to put UX in the context of numerical goals. Any of the metrics discussed in Chapter 2 can be used as the basis for an ROI estimate. All you need is a means of converting these figures into a dollar value.

Say your research surveys and usability tests of your prototype suggest that changes to the registration process will increase signups by 2000 users a week. Find out how much a registered user is worth to the business financially (your marketing team is a good place to start), multiply the two figures, and you have a ballpark ROI figure. It's crude, but it's a reasonable attempt at predicting design's value. Alternatively, you can build ROI cases by discussing cost savings that result from UX design. A well-designed site can theoretically reduce the need for customer-service support, or a well-designed content-upload process could free up the time of employees who would otherwise be adding content manually. Be cautious with ROI derived from cost savings. It is easy to invent spurious calculations that assume a world without human limitations, where every second saved is directed back toward profitable business. No organization works this way, and smart business owners will see through a case built on this premise.

UX designers can end up wasting their youth chasing ROI figures when they'd be better off designing. It's easier to show your intentions through a makeshift prototype than through an elaborate business plan. You're not there to be a numbers person; the business can hire more of those if needed. Although some businesses take a hard-line stance on ROI ("If it can't be measured, it doesn't count"), UX design isn't just about reducing risk or increasing conversion. It helps businesses do things that their customers love. It makes lives better. These intangibles matter, and businesses that live purely by the numbers lead a sadly blinkered life.

Whatever your approach to ROI, don't make promises you can't keep. ROI predictions are just that; don't let them become guarantees. Every individual design project is a gamble: it may succeed or it may fail. However, businesses that put long-term faith in design outperform those that don't. Research from the United Kingdom's Design Council shows that shares in design-led businesses have outperformed the FTSE 100 Index by more than 200 percent over the past decade. Convince your stakeholders that UX is a marathon, not a sprint, and explain that long-term investment will demonstrate a clear reward.

Tell stories

Where numbers fall short, stories offer a compelling way to describe the value of design. These could be tales from user research, or case studies of how UX has made a difference for other companies. They could relate mishaps you've had on other websites, or cautionary tales about failed launches that cost thousands of dollars. Your aim is to tell stories in which UX is the centerpiece. A story, like a good joke, is a way to captivate people's attention without fear of being interrupted. Memorable stories linger in the audience's minds.

Keep an eye out for great UX stories and practice recounting them. Once you've learned a few that illustrate your most important UX messages, look for the right moment to weave your magic.

Build your skills

Staying up-to-date is essential for your growth and credibility. Successful designers are insatiably curious about not only their specific medium but also the broader aspects of design. UX, like many web disciplines, is notable for its openness, and many renowned practitioners share their expertise generously. Don't hesitate to take advantage of the books, blogs, and case studies they offer. Cheap (and not-so-cheap) conferences and courses are perfect for brushing up on your UX expertise and offer valuable networking opportunities. Look around for events near you or, if there aren't any nearby, how about putting one on yourself?

Professional organizations such as the Information Architecture Institute (www.iainstitute.org) and Interaction Design Association (www.ixda.org) offer access to voluntary mentors. Mentoring schemes provide an excellent way to build your expertise with the knowledge and guidance of a seasoned practitioner. This relationship can prove particularly useful for undercover UX designers, who may not receive this level of specialized support from their line manager.

The user experience industry is notorious for desperately circular arguments about definitions, job titles, and how the various UX roles overlap. We won't open that can of worms, but as your career and responsibilities progress, you should consider your route within the field.

The so-called T-model, developed by Peter Boersma, senior experience designer at Adaptive Path, describes UX as the umbrella term joining a number of related disciplines. Within this model we see three potential shapes for a UX practitioner.

The generalist **A** has a grounding in all areas of UX practice.

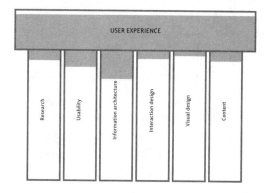

A *The generalist has a fair knowledge of all UX disciplines.*

The specialist **B** focuses on a single discipline and will probably hold the discipline's job title.

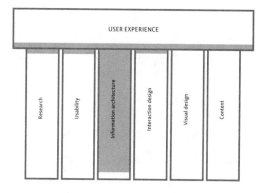

B *The specialist focuses on a specific discipline, in this case information architecture.*

Finally, the T-shaped practitioner **C** is a hybrid of both generalist and specialist, possessing deep knowledge of one or more fields but backing that up with good overall appreciation of other UX domains.

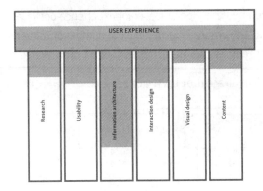

C *The "T-shaped" UX practitioner combines depth and breadth.*

In your undercover days you'll probably draw on techniques from across the UX spectrum, but as you progress, you may prefer to focus on a single discipline such as information architecture, usability, interaction design, or content strategy. All routes can be rewarding and full of opportunity; ultimately, your skills, interests, and company's needs should determine which route and job title suits you.

★ UX LEADERSHIP

Although high-quality design is valuable whatever the organization's current attitude to UX, to climb to the top rungs of the adoption ladder, the business must also see UX as a strategic force. You may eventually face the decision of remaining a pure UX practitioner or leading a team that can reposition UX at the heart of the business's strategy. By definition, UX leadership isn't undercover, but knowing the ropes will help you decide if it's the right path for you.

The point at which your organization needs more UX resources will likely be incontrovertible. If, as a full-time UX specialist, you're struggling to keep your head above water, it's time to look at getting some help. For a self-contained project, external consultants or freelancers might fit the bill, but if your needs are more long-term and strategic, you should consider building a team.

MANAGEMENT AND LEADERSHIP

Although many people use the words *management* and *leadership* interchangeably, they represent different roles. As head of a UX team, you will juggle both.

As a manager, you will take responsibility for the well-being and productivity of your employees. You'll spend a lot of time looking at process, making sure your team is involved at the right points, and eliminating hurdles so that your team can work unhindered. You'll focus on tactical issues such as estimation and project planning, as well as evaluating and motivating your staff.

As a leader, you will focus on the quality of your team's work, and how the business approaches UX design. You'll spend as much time looking up the organization chart as down it, seeking ways to improve the status of UX and helping the business use design strategically to produce better products and services. Your aim will be to infect the rest of the business with the UX bug, while continuing to cultivate it within your team.

Most people naturally lean toward either management or leadership. Whatever your bias, you shouldn't lose sight of either goal. It is easy to focus too much on either tactical management or visionary leadership, and a deficiency in either can lead to an unhappy work environment.

THE NATURE OF DESIGN LEADERSHIP

The demands of design leadership can be a shock. You'll spend more time in meetings and less time designing than you'd like. You'll have to protect your team from bad decisions and occasionally be forced to go along with them. You'll spend a great deal of time educating senior managers about the nature of design and learning how to communicate in the language of business. You may find it a lonely and thankless task, or you may find that the rewards of championing UX at a senior level (not to mention the extra pay) more than compensate for the downsides.

Some designers first move into a half-and-half role, such as lead or senior user experience designer, that combines some frontline design with managing a small team and leading the company's UX efforts. This can prove a successful and rewarding progression, but be aware that the role can lack stability. In a growing organization, team expansion will inevitably demand a full-time leader.

THE TEAM MAKEUP

The size and structure of your team will be driven by your needs. One approach is to assemble a team of specialists such as a user researcher, an information architect, and an interaction designer **D**.

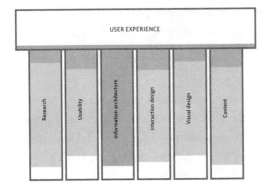

D Specialists can combine their individual skills, creating a team with genuine depth.

Specialist employees potentially bring deeper knowledge and more thorough processes, but the lack of overlap between the roles can leave the team stretched when workloads are imbalanced or a team member leaves.

On the other hand, a team of UX generalists **E** offers homogeneity, reliability, and flexibility.

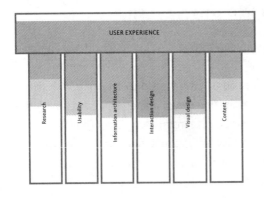

E A team of generalists has more overlap in skills and therefore can be more flexible.

This setup is often seen in agencies. With all team members covering similar territory, the team can be smaller, but unless you have exceptional employees, you may not achieve the levels of expertise and performance of the specialist model.

Your ability to recruit suitable staff will be affected by your location, remuneration, and the state of the market. At the time of writing, skilled mid- and senior-level practitioners are in short supply, while the growth of university courses in UX, human-computer interaction, and similar fields is generating many promising junior candidates. While experience is understandably desirable, a recent graduate could offer a great deal to your fledgling UX team at far lower cost than an experienced practitioner. In turn, you can share your undercover skills to help such employees put their academic knowledge into practice. Wherever you look, spend time finding the right people. The difference between a good and bad team member is startling.

As well as the right talent, you'll also need a comfortable home in the organization chart. UX teams often report to marketing departments, product teams, or, in smaller companies, IT teams that have responsibility for the website. Another possibility, less commonly seen, is to locate UX within customer service departments, since both groups naturally share the user-centered mindset. Finally, a UX team that reports to senior managers or even the chief executive is ideally placed for strategic influence, although this is unlikely to happen until your organization reaches the integrated UX adoption phase. Chapter 6 helps you understand the practicalities of these potential relationships.

MANAGING UX STAFF

User experience designers are an interesting bunch to manage. While the individuals you work with may possess widely differing personalities, UX designers commonly share a number of values and traits.

A strain of benevolent ambition can often be seen throughout the UX industry. Many practitioners feel driven by the duty to make the world a better place, meaning they entertain far-reaching goals of making a genuine difference. These goals can match and even surpass the usual motivations of money and status (although UX people appreciate pay and recognition as much as anyone else). An organization that demonstrates clear values is likely to appeal to a UX designer, since the values illuminate an unspoken understanding of the likely work environment.

UX designers are by their nature interested in people, but this empathy doesn't necessarily translate into extroversion. UX folk can be thoughtful and even quiet. Since UX designers are as much at home with abstract ideas and processes as with detail, a leader must appreciate the difference between productivity and visible output. Your employee may spend all day deep in thought with no obvious end result, but finally reach an essential mental breakthrough. Alternatively, she may spend a day churning out deliverables that she has been unable to put any productive thought into. A 20th-century industrial management style that measures a day's work only by the artifacts it creates is not a good fit for a UX team.

Like most knowledge workers, UX designers are typically motivated by autonomy, guidance, and feedback. However, remember that autonomy without direction frustrates employees as much as micromanagement. As a leader, you must explain where the goalposts lie and what you expect from your employees, and then step back to allow them to respond in their own way. If your employees are performing well and are eager to grow, they will be easy to lead. However, if a team member's performance or motivation slips, you should step closer into either a coaching role or, where necessary, corrective supervision. The UX adoption curve can throw up disappointment and failure as much as success, meaning UX designers sometimes need the support of a good leader to revive their motivation.

Finally, try to create an environment in which your employees can learn. Designers are strongly motivated by personal growth, and once your employees believe they can no longer learn anything useful from their role, they already have one foot out the door. Look for ways to bring external knowledge to your team (through books, conferences, or perhaps invited guests), and strive to share UX knowledge among the team. If possible, experiment on every new project. New approaches keep minds fresh, and you might just find a better way to work.

★ MOVING ON

For some designers, a leadership role offers the opportunity to make a lasting impact, while reaping the benefits of status and reward. For others, the very idea is torture. Many people in the industry love the practitioner's life too deeply to consider ever leaving the front lines, meaning their main career choices are where to work and how long to stay.

We know that some of our readers will see only a limited future with their current employer. Although the undercover tactics in this book have worked for us and many others, your company may never appreciate UX design the way you do. Sometimes UX adoption can only be driven by a role you can't fulfill, and your efforts will be fruitless. Put bluntly, sometimes it's better to quit.

It may seem odd that a book on how to sneak UX into your business is now giving advice on how to give up, but we believe the industry is best served by happy, productive practitioners. While watching UX design gain traction in a company can be fantastically rewarding, the undercover life is tough, and the appeal of a design-literate organization with a thriving UX team can be strong.

Of course, only you can choose the time to move on. Are you happy in your work? Are you able to use your skills effectively? Are you growing as a designer? Entrepreneur and author Seth Godin once claimed, "The time to look for a new job is when you don't need one." For Godin, once you're pigeonholed in a company, you'll be forever limited by others' expectations. Not all of us are brave enough to follow this bold advice, but within it lies a clear truth: sometimes you need to step sideways for a better jump. It can be difficult to persuade a company to create a full-time UX position for you, particularly if the company is struggling for resources. You can appeal to the company's prudence, explaining it will be cheaper to train you than hire an external UX professional, but sometimes it's best to take the company as far you can, build a portfolio, and apply elsewhere. It's what we call "the legitimizing move"—the one that gives you the job title, the pay rise, or at least the reassurance that you're finally a full-fledged UX designer.

The legitimizing move can work, and in some companies it might be your only option. However, it shouldn't be used as an easy escape route if you're afraid of putting in the effort. Conceding defeat too early demonstrates only laziness, and the grass may not be so green once you reach the other side. However, recruiters appreciate that, with few designers in our young field having formal UX qualifications, many candidates are moving into the industry from related fields such as development, visual design, or marketing. These recruiters will demand evidence that you have successfully taken a role as far as it can go. If, for example, you have lifted your organization from undercover to emergent UX, you probably have what it takes. If you gave up prematurely, perhaps you don't.

YOUR NEW ROLE

Your ideal role will depend on many personal factors such as salary requirements, location, age, and aspirations. We can't advise you on those, but we can offer some thoughts on one of the most fundamental debates: innie versus outtie.

As an in-house designer at an organization with mature UX processes, you'll get stuck into detailed, rewarding work, develop strong relationships with the business and its stakeholders, and be part of a company that values UX through and through. You'll work thoroughly on a small number of sites or applications, research user behavior in depth, and be able to demonstrate measurable value from your work.

As an external consultant, you'll work with a wide variety of clients, building up a broad portfolio, and learning about numerous business sectors. You'll excel at working fast while drawing on the skills of fellow consultants, and learn to communicate a persuasive case for your work.

Your preference is likely to be highly personal, but engage both your brain and your heart when making the innie-outtie decision. Making the switch between the two sides can be more difficult than it appears. Although one side might be a more comfortable fit, a UX designer can learn a great deal by sampling both in-house and external work. Whatever your role, having experience of the scenarios, methods, and culture of the other side of the coin will make you a stronger designer.

RÉSUMÉS AND PORTFOLIOS

As with any job, you should first make the right connections when looking for a new UX role. The more senior you are, the more likely you'll hear of vacancies through your personal network rather than through third-party sources, but whatever your position in the market, you will rely on the same two documents: the résumé and the portfolio.

Your résumé is of course your chance to explain your employment history and how you've made a difference. The usual advice applies: keep it short, omit irrelevant detail, and confidently explain your skills and what you can bring to a role. If you are new to the field, your résumé should demonstrate your aptitude—do you have the major skills required of a full-time UX designer? At more senior levels, recruiters will assume you know the fundamental techniques of UX. Here, your résumé should describe your attitude—that is, your underlying approach to design, and the methods by which you've succeeded elsewhere.

An up-to-date résumé isn't only useful if you're after a new job. Reviewing your résumé every few months will force you to focus on the benefits you've brought to your organization, replenishing your ammunition for making the case for UX.

Your portfolio is the "how" to your résumé's "what." It explains how you have tackled UX design challenges throughout your career, and casts light upon your thought processes. Don't use your portfolio just to show off your deliverables or the finished product. Anyone can make a wireframe. But few people can accurately demonstrate the UX techniques—from research through ideas to deliverables to iteration—that accompanied it. A portfolio should therefore contain examples of your work from all phases of the UX design process: personas, sketches, sitemaps, A/B test results, usability test reports, tree test statistics, wireflows—you name it. Focus, however, on quality above quantity. Every page should illustrate your skilled approach to UX design.

Be honest about your role in both your résumé and portfolio. If you squeezed some undercover UX improvements into an existing design process, say so. You'll show maturity by recognizing the value that others bring, and you'll only create a noose for your own neck if the interviewer asks for details of a project in which you weren't deeply involved.

Building up a reasonable UX portfolio shouldn't be difficult. The techniques in this book will create plenty of diagrams, drawings, and documents that show your approach. Be sure to respect confidentiality by keeping deliverables anonymous and carefully selecting what you include. If you really can't show anything from your current role, you may have to create extra portfolio pieces in your spare time. Help your friends with their websites, make process flows for existing applications, or even contribute to volunteer projects. Open-source software is often in desperate need of UX help, but be aware that developers and community contributors may have invested a great deal of personal pride in the project.

★ OVER TO YOU

Whether you choose to stay put or move on, many paths lie at your feet. Although the world is slowly recognizing the user experience cause, our field is still finding its way, and the next few years will herald a fresh set of challenges. We'll have to fall in step with the incessant march of the web beyond the desktop onto cellphones, tablet computers, and games consoles, and learn to create unified experiences across devices. We'll have to handle fierce competition as other businesses realize it's no longer enough to compete purely on features or price. We'll have to design sustainably to conserve our diminishing natural resources. It won't be easy, but making a difference never is.

The undercover manifesto and the techniques we've covered should point you in the right direction on your journey. You'll need to be realistic, resilient, and irrepressible. A pragmatic attitude will shield you from the frustration and disappointment that comes from demanding perfection. That's not to say it will be an easy ride. The most effective designers are those who obsess over their craft. Expect to work hard and taste both sweet success and glorious failure.

The good news is that you aren't alone, although at times it may feel that way. There are thousands of people facing the same journey; seek out your local UX community to swap stories and contribute to the discussion. Keep learning and keep your head up, and you'll find the undercover UX mission interesting and rewarding. Because of people like you, organizations across the world are starting to understand the benefits of putting people first, and the world is becoming a little more enjoyable as a result.

The rest is up to you. There's no way to guarantee excellent design. Although we hope you've learned some useful approaches among these pages, you must find out what methods work for your style, your company, and your users. A book is a tinderbox for ideas, and we hope that you embrace, twist, and ignore our thoughts to suit your needs. Experiment to see what works, making the most of your successes and learning from your failures. Let us know how you get on, and we hope in turn you'll pass on your undercover wisdom to others.

WHERE NEXT?: FURTHER READING

- *Influence: The Psychology of Persuasion*, by Robert B. Cialdini (Collins Business Essentials, 2007)

- *Storytelling for User Experience: Crafting Stories for Better Design*, by Whitney Quesenbery and Kevin Brooks (Rosenfeld Media, 2010)

- *Information Architecture for the World Wide Web, 3rd Edition*, by Louis Rosenfeld and Peter Morville (O'Reilly, 2006)

- *The UX Leadership Journal*, www.uxleadership.com

- "Time to Quit?" by Seth Godin, http://sethgodin.typepad.com/seths_blog/2006/06/time_to_quit.html

- "T-Model: Big IA Is Now UX," by Peter Boersma, http://beep.peterboersma.com/2004/11/t-model-big-ia-is-now-ux.html

- "Specialists Versus Generalists: A False Dichotomy?" by Pabini Gabriel-Petit, http://www.uxmatters.com/mt/archives/2009/02/specialists-versus-generalists-a-false-dichotomy.php

INDEX

CSS, 86, 87, 92
cultural factors, 19–23
customer feedback. *See* user feedback
customer research. *See* user research
customer satisfaction, 14
customer-service application, 124
customer-service representives, 30
customer surveys, 29

D
deadlines, 21–22
deliverables, 70–95
  defined, 70
  fidelity considerations, 81–89
  functional specifications, 80–81
  making better, 90–95
  page description diagrams, 78–79
  prototypes, 77, 79–80, 82, 86
  recommended books on, 95
  role of, 70–71
  sitemaps, 71–73
  tailoring for audience, 88
  updating, 89, 98
  user flows, 73–76
  wireframes, 76–77
demographic information, 36
design by committee, 21
Design Consequences game, 58–59
design critiques. *See* critiques
design deliverables. *See* deliverables
design disinterest, 20
design games, 54–61
Designing for the Digital Age, 40
Designing Interfaces, 95
Designing with Web Standards, 92, 157
design leadership, 169
design mockups, 86
design objectives, 14
design pattern libraries, 90–91
design principles, 64–66
design problems, 13–23
  and cultural factors, 19–23
  defining, 13
  framing, 14–15
  researching the business, 16–19
  subjectivity of, 15
design process. *See also* UX design
  collaborating on, 51–61
  complexity of, 13
  fluid nature of, 132
  generating ideas for, 42–43, 61
  recommended books on, 67
  role of critiques in, 113
  role of deliverables in, 70–71 (*See also* deliverables)
  sustaining momentum for, 62
design research, 143
design reviews, 113–114. *See also* critiques
Design the Box game, 54–56
Design with Intent Toolkit, 61

design workshops, 52–54, 62
desktop software, 4
developers, 132–136
diary studies, 32
direct observation, 29
divergent thinking, 42–43, 61
drawing tools, 46–47
Dreamweaver, 86
drop shadows, 48
dummy text, 94
dynamic pages, 149

E
EightShapes, 78
emergent UX phase, 160
entry pages, 9
Essential Persona Lifecycle, The, 40
Ethnio, 109
Excel, 72
exclusions, 15
executive summaries, 33–34
expectations, 21
expert reviews, 6–7, 8

F
face-to-face interviews, 27–28
feature requests, 15, 30, 160
feedback, 120, 124, 127. *See also* user feedback
Feedback Army, 111
fidelity, 81–89
figures, drawing, 49–50
Fireworks, 84, 86
"first-run" experience, 93
Fitts' Law, 122
FiveSecondTest, 111
Flash Catalyst, 86
Flash Professional, 86
Fletcher, Alan, 61, 67
Flickr, 92
fly-on-the-wall technique, 29
focus groups, 28, 30
formative testing, 100
form shadows, 48
Fried, Jason, 157
functional specifications, 80–81
FY Threshold, 122

G
Gabriel-Petit, Pabini, 177
games, design, 54–61
Gamestorming, 67
GarageBand, 27
Garrett, Jesse James, 72
generalists, user experience, 167, 170, 177
Get Satisfaction, 124
Getting Real: The Smarter, Faster, Easier Way to Build a Successful Web Application, 157
gift certificates, 110
Godin, Seth, 173, 177
Goodwin, Kim, 40